FLYNN'S FAMILY AND FRIEND'S COOKBOOK

LORIA FLYNN
AND AMIRA FLYNN

BALBOA.PRESS
A DIVISION OF HAY HOUSE

Balboa Press books may be ordered through booksellers or by contacting:

Balboa Press
A Division of Hay House
1663 Liberty Drive
Bloomington, IN 47403
www.balboapress.com
844-682-1282

Because of the dynamic nature of the Internet, any web addresses or links contained in this book may have changed since publication and may no longer be valid. The views expressed in this work are solely those of the author and do not necessarily reflect the views of the publisher, and the publisher hereby disclaims any responsibility for them.

The author of this book does not dispense medical advice or prescribe the use of any technique as a form of treatment for physical, emotional, or medical problems without the advice of a physician, either directly or indirectly. The intent of the author is only to offer information of a general nature to help you in your quest for emotional and spiritual well-being. In the event you use any of the information in this book for yourself, which is your constitutional right, the author and the publisher assume no responsibility for your actions.

Any people depicted in stock imagery provided by Getty Images are models, and such images are being used for illustrative purposes only. Certain stock imagery © Getty Images.

Print information available on the last page.

ISBN: 978-1-9822-7163-3 (sc)
ISBN: 978-1-9822-7165-7 (hc)
ISBN: 978-1-9822-7164-0 (e)

Library of Congress Control Number: 2021914437

Balboa Press rev. date: 07/24/2021

CONTENTS

APPETIZERS & BEVERAGES

SOUPS & SALDAS

VEGETABLES

MAIN DISH

BREAD & ROLLS

DESSERTS

THIS & THAT

COOKIES & CANDY

THIS AND THAT / MISCELLANEOUS

OTHER RECIPES

FAMILY PICTURES

APPETIZERS & BEVERAGES

Salsa

Loria Flynn

4 Lg. tomatoes chopped.
½ onion, chopped.
½ green chili pepper, chopped.
½ jalapeno, chopped.
½ c. cilantro, chopped.
½ green pepper, chopped.
1 clove garlic, chopped.
1 tsp. white vinegar
1 tsp. sugar

Mix all ingredients together, salt and pepper to taste, chill or do not.

For the Garden of Your Daily Living

Carroll Ann Tolleson

Plant three of peas:
1.peace of mind
2.peace of heart
3.peace of soul
Plant four rows of squash
Squash gossip
Squash indifference
Squash grumbling
Squash selfishness
Plant four rows of lettuce:
1.lettuce be faithful
2. lettuce be kind
3.lettuce be patient
4.lettuce really love one another
No garden without turnips:
Turnip for meetings
Turnip for service
Turnip to help one another.
To conclude our garden must have thyme:
1.thyme for each other
2. thyme for family
3. thyme for friends

Water freely with pittance and cultivate with love there is much fruit in your garden because you reap what you sow.

Reception Punch

Loria Flynn

6 c. water
4 c. sugar
1 (16 oz.) can frozen orange concentrate
1 (6 oz.) can frozen lemonade concentrate
1 (46 oz.) can pineapple juice
¼ c. lemon juice
3 mashed bananas'
2 qts. Ginger ale

Boil water and sugar for 3 mins. Till sugar dissolves. Add remaining ingredients except ginger ale mix well and freeze thaw until slushy and slowly add ginger ale.

Easy Enchanted Punch

Loria Flynn

8 c. cranberry juice
6 c. apple cider
1 lt. ginger ale
1 tray of ice cubes
Cinnamon sticks
Orange slices

Pour cranberry juice and apple cider into large bowl. Break the cinnamon sticks in half. Put one-piece cinnamon stick in each hole in ice cube tray and 1 piece of orange, fill ice tray with cranberry apple mix. Freeze and refrigerate remaining punch mix. In bowl before serving add ginger ale and ice juice

Pumpkin Punch Bowl

Loria Flynn

2 glow in the dark sticks
1 lg. pumpkin
1 heat resistant punch bowl that will fit inside the pumpkin.

Hollow out pumpkin and carve a design in it place punch bowl inside pumpkin right before the party begins. Activate glow sticks put in pumpkin before the bowl and add enchanted punch.

Bloody Mary

Loria Flynn

13 ½ oz. can tomato juice.
1 Tbsp. spoon Worcestershire Sauce
1 Tbsp. Lemon Juice
1 tsp. salt
¼ tsp. tobacco sauce

Add ground black pepper to taste.
Mix well.

Witches Brew

Loria Flynn

1 gl. Apple cider
1 orange
1 apple
3 cinnamon sticks
⅛ tsp. nutmeg
1 handful rose petals.
1 big pot

Pour apple cider into lg. kettle Pell orange and squeeze juice into cider, discarding the pulp. tear the orange Pell into 1 in. strips and add to mix. Core apple and cut into ¼ in. slices add to mix. Break the cinnamon sticks in half add to mix. Add nutmeg warm over low heat for 2 hrs. do not boil.

Frosty fruit cooler

Loria Flynn

3 c. apricot nectar, chilled
3 c. pineapple or orange juice chilled
1 qt. ginger ale
1 pt. pineapple or orange sherbet

In punch bowl, combine apricot nectar and pineapple juice just before serving add sherbet and ginger ale.

Eggnog milkshake

Loria Flynn

1 Tbsp. sugar
Dash salt
1 c. milk
½ tsp. vanilla
½ tsp. rum extract
1 scoop vanilla ice cream
nutmeg

in blender or sm. bowl, combine first 5 ingredients mix until frothy
then add rest and mix well.

Lemon Cheese

Loria Flynn

⅔ c. melted butter.
1 c. sugar
2 Tbsp. grated lemon rind
½ c. lemon juice
3 eggs
4 egg yolks

Combine butter, sugar, lemon rind and juice in top of double boiler, blend well. Beat eggs and egg yolks together until light and frothy. stir eggs into lemon mixture, cook over hot water, stirring constantly until thickened. Pour into small jars and cool. Lemon cheese will keep for weeks stored in refrigerator.

Party Mix

Loria Flynn

2 c. oat cereal

3 c. rice squares cereal

2 c. bite sized shredded wheat cereal

1 c. peanuts, pecans or cashews

1 c. thin pretzel sticks

½ c. butter melted.

4 Tbsp. Worcestershire sauce

Dash of tabasco sauce

½ tsp. seasoned salt

½ tsp. garlic salt

½ tsp. onion salt

Combine cereals, nuts and pretzels in slow cooker. Mix remaining ingredients.

Pour over cereal mixture and toss lightly to coat. Do not cover slow cooker.

Cook on high for 2 hrs., stirring well every 30 min, then turn to low for 2 – 6 hrs.

Store in airtight container.

Party Mix
Loria Flynn

1 bag peanuts
1 bag m & m's
1 Bag of other nuts
1 box check mixes cereal

Mix with season salt onion and garlic powder. Mix well and server warm.

Popcorn balls

Loria Flynn

1 bottle of white corn syrup
Marsh mellow cream,
Butter

Take a bottle of white corn syrup, marshmallow cream, butter, mix popcorn syrup.

Butter and marshmallow together. Put in a cake pan, coated in butter and fridge tell set up and serve.

People Puppy Chow
Loria Flynn

½ c. peanut butter
¼ c. butter (½ stick)
11 ½ oz pkg. milk chocolate chips
8 c. crispy cereal
1 ½ c. powdered sugar

Melt in lg. saucepan, first 3 ingredients then mix cereal and shake all up in Ziplock bags. With powdered sugar. Put on cookie sheet, to cool.

SOUPS & SALDAS

Chili Wheels

10 burrito size flour tortillas
8 oz sour cream
8 oz cream cheese
2 sm. Cans chopped green chilies.
½ tsp. garlic powder
½ lb. shredded ham

Mix all ingredients (except for tortillas) refrigerate 2 hrs. spared on tortillas.

Roll up refrigerate overnight slice into about ¾ in. pieces.

Snowball Salad

Margaret Ralls

1 ½ c. sugar
1 c sour cream
2 Tbsp. lemon juice
2 (9oz.) cool whip
1 lg. can crush pineapple drained.
2 c. maraschino cherries

Mix to ingredients together, then fold in the rest of them. Serve frozen or chilled.

Ice Cream Salad

Ione Brown

2 pkgs strawberry Jell-O
2 c. boiling water
1-pint vanilla ice cream
1 c. crushed pineapple
1 c. chopped nuts.
1 c. diced celery

Dissolve 2 pkgs. Strawberry Jell-O in 2 c. boiling water. While still hot add 1-pint vanilla ice cream, stir in 1 c. crushed nuts and 1 c. diced celery let set and serve.

Fruit Salad

Vernice Boyd

2 boxes pineapple Jell-O
2 boxes orange Jell-O
2 c. boiling water
4 c. of vanilla ice cream
1 c. coconut
½ c. crushed pineapple

Mix all ingredients keep in ice box until ready to serve.

5 Minute Luncheon Salad

Ione Brown

1 c. (Flat) crushed pineapple
1 box strawberry Jell-O
1 sm. 12oz. carton cottage cheese
1 sm. Carton cool whip
1 c. nuts (optional)

Ina small saucepan, heat 1 can flat crushed pineapple just long enough to dissolve a small pkg. of strawberry Jell-O while you stir remove from heat and mix in 1 sm. Carton cottage cheese.

Fold 1 sm. Carton cool whip to the mixture nuts maybe add nut if desired. Serve at once or can be stored in refrigerator.

Cranberry Salad

Reba Quetone

½ c. sugar
2 c. ground raw cranberries
1 c. tokay grapes halved and seeded.
½ c. nuts
6 lg. marsh mellows cut in ¼.
½ c. whipped cream

Ground cranberries with coarsest knife in food chopper, Add sugar to cranberries place in refrigerator to chill. Drain adds grapes, nuts and marshmallow's, fold in whip cream just before serving in a crisp lettuce leaf.

Coke Salad

Odessa St. John

2pkg. 3oz.blackberry Jell-O
1 c. dark sweet cherries (pitted)
1 sm. Can crushed pineapple.
1 c. pecans
2 c. coke

Drain juice from cherries and pineapple, add enough water to make 2 c. liquid.

Heat liquid dissolve in Jell-O let cool, add coke chill and add fruit and nuts.

Clam Chowder

Reva Hensley

3 slices of bacon (raw)
1 c. diced celery
1 c. chopped onions.
2 c. minced clams
1 lb. or 2 c. potatoes
1 c. diced carrots
½ tsp. salt
¼ tsp. Thyme
Dash pepper

Cook bacon, add celery and onions and cook partially. Drain clams reserve liquor. Add water to make 4 c. add to bacon mix, add rest of ingredients cover and simmer 35 min. blend 2 Tbsp. flour 3 Tbsp. water to make a paste stir and bring to simmer again.

Hot Ham Salad

Margaret Ralls

2 c. chopped ham.
2 c. cooked rice
¾ c. chopped celery.
1 ¼ c. miracle whip
¾ c. rice krispies

Mix the above ingredients spread into a baking dish. sprinkle top with rice krispies about ¾ c.

Top with your favorite cheese (grated) bake at 350 about 25 min.

Brussel Sport Soup

Reva Hensley

2 pkg frozen Brussel sprouts
5 C. Chicken Broth
¼ c. margarine
½ c. flour
1 c. dairy powder cream
¼ tsp. white pepper
½ tsp. salt

Cook sprouts, add 2 c. broth and place in blender (drain) puree, melt butter add flour. Cook 1 min. add creamer boil and thicken add puree.

Macaroni Salad

Reva Hensley

1 pkg, macaroni
1 lg. can tuna
1 bag or box frozen peas
1 sm. Can chopped black olives.
1 lg. onion chopped.
1 bunch green onions
1 c. celery chopped.
Shredded cheese
1 tsp. white pepper

Cook macaroni let cool then mix above with mayo keep in refrigerator till ready to serve.

White House Salad

Ouida Boyd

1 extra lg. cool whip
1 lg. can cherry pie filling
1 c. eagle brand cream
1 c. chopped pecans.
303 can crushed pineapple.

Combine all above ingredients chill and serve.

7-layer Salad

Reva Hensley

1 head of lettuce chopped.
4 stalks celery chopped.
½ c. dried onion
1 sm. green pepper chopped.
1 pkg. sour cream
½ pint mayo
10 strips of bacon cooked and crumbed.
Parmesan cheese
3 Tbsp. sugar

Mix all together serve.

Macaroni Tuna Salad   Martha Pannell

1 pkg. shell macaroni
2 cans tuna
½ lb. sharp cheddar cheese chopped.
6 boiled eggs
1 bunch green onions
2 celery stocks chopped.
1 bell pepper(green) chopped.
1 bell Pepper(red) chopped.

Cook macaroni according to directions chop and add all the ingredients add mayo and salt and pepper to taste.

Green Bean Salad

Ouida Boyd

1 c. cut green beans - drained.

Sm. can pimentos - drained

1 c. chopped celery.

1 med. Onion chopped.

1 med. green bell pepper chopped.

Dressing:

¼ c. sugar

1 Tbsp. salt

½ tsp. pepper

¼ c. salad oil

½ c. vinegar

1 Tbsp. water

Pour dressing over vegetable mixture, refrigerate overnight.

Cornbread Salad

Carroll Ann Tolleson

1 - 6oz. pkg.
½ c. chopped onion.
½ c. green peppers
½ c. chopped cherry tomatoes.
¼ c. light miracle whip
¼ c. cucumber ranch dressing
½ tsp. salt
2 Tbsp. mustard

Cook jiffy cornbread mix, crumble in large bowl, add onions, green peppers, tomatoes, to mix. Blend remaining ingredients in small bowl. pour over cornbread mixture and mix well.

Broccoli Salad

Donna Murphy

5 c. broccoli
½ c. gold raisins
8 slices cooked chopped bacon.
1 sm. onion chopped.

Dressing:
1 c, mayo (the real stuff)
¼ c. sugar
3 Tbsp. vinegar

Mix all chill and serve.

German Potato Salad

Teresa Murphy

Potatoes
2 onions chopped.
½ tsp. celery seeds
4 strips bacon
2 tsp. flour
½ c. vinegar
1 Tbsp. sugar
½ c. water
Salt
Pepper

Boil potatoes with jackets on cut in cubes.

Mix all ingredients chill and serve.

Beet Jell-O Salad

Reva Hensley

1 pack lemon jell -0
1 c. warm water
¾ c. beet juice
¾ c. celery
3 Tbsp. Vinegar
½ tsp. salt
2 Tbsp. onion juice
1 Tbsp. horseradish
1 c. cooked beets diced.

Dissolves jell – o in warm water add beet juice, vinegar, salt, onion juice, horseradish, chill. when slightly thickened.

Fold in celery and beets

turn into a mold or other dish chill.

Watergate Salad

Al Miller

1 carton 9 oz. whip topping
1 box instant pistachio pudding
1 can (# 1) crushed pineapple and juice
1 c. mini marshmallow's
½ c. nuts

Fold dry pudding mix into whip topping add pineapple, juice, marshmallows and nuts mix all refrigerate.

Slaw

Carroll Ann Tolleson

2 lg. carrots grated.

2 green bell pepper finely chopped.

2 yellow onions finely chopped.

2 lbs. cabbage grated.

2c. sugar

Put in gl. Jar.

bring following to a rolling boil:

1 c. vinegar

1 c. oil

2 Tbsp. salt

2 Tbsp. celery seed

Pour over veggies stir well cover and put in refrigerator for 24 hrs. before serving.

I Really Must Go Shopping Today

For one thing, I am all out of TOLERANCE and I cannot seem to function very well without it. Also, my supply of GENEROITY has run low and I want to get some before it is all gone. I must exchange SELF-SATISFACTION I picked last week foe some HUMILITY; it is supposed to ware so much better, and I noticed my PATIENCE has gotten short; I saw a longer style on a friend last week and I thought it very becoming my since of humor needs repairing and if I can match the KINDESS I saw the other day, I would like to have some of that too.

The MORALS look shaky right now, so I guess I will keep my old ones, and everyone says LOVE is hard to find these days that I really should share my supply with those less fortunate than I. How quickly the "goods" in our lives are lost, misplaced or depleted…. Yes… I really must go shopping today.

Cornbread salad

Donna Wells

2 boxes of Jeff cornbread mix
1 bell pepper, chopped.
1 onion, chopped.
1 lb. bacon cooked and crumbled.
1 lg. tomato, chopped.
1 c. sour cream
1 c. ranch dressing
1 Celery stick, chopped.
1 lg. tomatoes

Fix corn bread as directed, cool crumble into container, while cooking bread fry bacon, pepper, celery and onions cook in bacon drippings.

Layer cornbread, bell pepper, onion, bacon and tomatoes. In a separate bowl, mix sour cream and ranch dressing together. Spread dressing in over top of salad. Refrigerate for at least 2 hrs. stir well before serving mixing it all up.

Broccoli Cauliflower supreme salad — Donna Wells

1 broccoli top
½ head cauliflower
1 c. broken pieces cashews
8 bacon slices crispy
1 can chestnuts slices, drained
1 can cashews

Diced tops of broccoli and cauliflower only the finest parts only. best red onion, cashews, crispy cooked bacon make sure to drain bacon and vegetables before putting in salad. mines the nuts into small pieces. Mix all vegetables together and put in refrigerator overnight. Suture every 2 hrs. to make sure the dressing coats all of salad, before you serve put nuts on it.

Green Pea Salad
Loria Flynn

1 can Green Peas
1 sm. Onion or 6 green onions
2 boiled eggs
¼ c. mayo
Dash garlic powder to taste
Dash salt to taste
Relish to taste

Open and drain peas, put in bowl mix in rest of ingredients tasting to see if enough garlic, salt, and relish.

Southwest Mexican layered salad

Loria Flynn

1 box jiffy cornbread mix
6 c. romaine lettuce
1 can shoe peg corn
1 c. salsa chunky halved
1 c. shredded Mexican blend cheese.
Dressing
Frito chips
Brown beef

1 box jiffy cornbread muffin mix.

Romaine lettuce 6 cups torn,15 oz. can black beans, drain and rinsed.

1 can shoe peg corn, drained layer this by half in order listed.
1 c. chunky salsa halved,
1 c. shredded Mexican blend cheese put another half on top layer same.

Cook and crumble 1 box of jiffy corn muffins mix and add more shredded cheese to taste.

Add half the dressing drizzled Surround the bowl with test of flavor chips or Frito scoops. I am an extra bowl of cheese and salsa dish on the table kind of person.

Serves 6 easily.

Pink lady salad

Loria Flynn

Cool whip lg. bowl
Fruit cocktail
Cherry Jell-O

Take cool whip and mix Jell-O just to make it pink mix drained fruit cocktail gently.

Mexican hat salad

Loria Flynn

Take all the peppers you can get.
9 different types of peppers
1 lg. onion
2 med. Tomatoes
1 Tbsp. vinegar
1 Tbsp. sugar
Dash of salt

Clean peppers get seeds out chop into small pieces. Clean and chop onion and tomatoes.

Mix all together 1 Tbsp. vinegar, 1 Tbsp. sugar, dash of salt.

Mix well, if to hot add more tomatoes to cool down.

Egg Salad

Loria Flynn

4 Boiled eggs

1 Tbsp. relish

1 tsp. mustard

2Tbsp. mayo

Dash Garlic

Dash salt

Dash pepper

Dash tabasco

Dash powder onion or finely chopped onion.

Mix well make sandwich.

Southern Potato Salad

Loria Flynn

Boil 5-10 potatoes
1 lg. onion
6 eggs boiled.
Relish
Mustard
Salt
Pepper
Sugar
Tabasco
Parsley
Garlic

Mix well cool and serve.

Boil patatas and eggs peel chop and mix with rest of ingredients cool
and serve.

Pink Lady Salad

Loria Flynn

Fruit cocktail
Bananas
Pears
Pineapple
Any other fruit you like.
Jell-O mix what flavor you like cherry, strawberry, etc.
Cool whip

Drain fruit put in bowl mix well cool whip and fruit together, add a little Jell-O powder to color the cool whip. Add 1 cup ice cream mix tell all is mixed well and all mix together.

Macaroni Salad

Marion Wilemon

¾ c. uncooked elbow macaroni
6 oz. can tuna
2 Tbsp. mayo
¼ Celery seed

Salad with dressing on the side

Peach Salad

Linda Head Driggers

1 can peach pie filling.

1 can pineapple chucks, drained

1 c green grapes

1 c. red grapes

3 bananas, dipped in lemon juice.

Mix all together and garnish with slices of kiwi fruit.

Watermelon Salad Mary Huckaby

¼ c. sugar
¼ c. chopped fresh mint.
½ tsp. ground ginger
1 med. Watermelon cut into 1 inch. Chunks
2 c. halves seedless grapes
Fresh mint leaves

Fruit salad:
1 pt. blueberries
1 pt. strawberries hulled and halved.

In small saucepan combine sugar, ¼ c. water, mint and ginger. Bring to boiling; reduce heat and simmer 5 mins. To thicken slightly. Set aside to cool.

Place watermelon, raspberries, blueberries, strawberries and grapes in lg. bowl. Add syrup mixture and toss to coat.

Top with mint leaves. (I do not like mint, so I do not use it.)

Cucumber Onion Salad
Loria Flynn & Charles Norton

2 English cucumbers peeled and thinly slices.
1 pt. cherry tomatoes or grape tomatoes, halved.
1 small green bell pepper, chopped.
1 medium sweet onion, chopped.
⅓ c. vegetable oil
¼ c. balsamic vinegar
2 Tbsp. capers
2 tsp. Italian seasoning or herbs

Combine cucumbers, tomatoes, bell pepper, and onion in a med. Bowl.

Whisk together oil, balsamic vinegar, capers, and Italian seasoning in a lg. bowl. Drizzle over cucumber mixture, tossing to coat.

Veggie Chicken Salad Squares   Loria Flynn

2 (8 oz.) pkg. refrigerated crescent roll dough.
1 (8 oz) cream cheese, softened
½ c. sour cream
1 tsp. dill weed.
¼ tsp. pepper
8 oz. shredded deli roasted chicken breast (2 c.)
½ c. crumbled blue cheese (2 oz.)
1 plum tomato, chopped.
⅓ c. shredded carrot
½ c. coarsely chopped roasted cashews.
2 Tbsp. chopped parsley.

Preheat oven to 375* place dough in single layer in ungreased baking pan. Press over bottom and up sides of pan. Bake 13 to 17 mins. Or until brown. Cool on wire rack at least 30 mins.

Meanwhile, in small bowl stir together cream cheese, sour cream, dill weed and pepper. Spread over cooled crust. Top with chicken, blue cheese, tomato and carrot. Lightly press toppings into cheese mixture. Sprinkle with cashews and parsley. Cut into squares, diamonds or triangles to serve. Serve immediately or cover and refrigerate up to 2 hrs.

Bacon and Broccoli Salad

Loria Flynn

1 lb. bacon, crisp-cooked, drained, and crumbled
2 heads broccoli, cut into bite-size pieces.
1 c. seedless red grapes, halves
1 c. light mayonnaise
½ c. granular sugar

In lg. skillet cook bacon until crisp. Drain on paper towels. Crumble and set aside.

In lg. bowl combine broccoli, reserved bacon, and grapes.

In small bowl stir together mayo and sugar. Add broccoli mix. Lightly toss until coated. Refrigerate until served.

Creamy fruit salad   Loria Flynn

2 c. cubed melons (cantaloupe, honeydew, or watermelon)
½ c. cubed apples
½ c. fresh blue berries
1 banana, sliced.
1 seedless orange peeled and cut up into cubes.
½ c. yogurt or pudding
1 tsp. grated orange peel
¼ tsp. nutmeg
3 Tbsp. nut if desired

In med bowl, combine the fruit. Combine pudding, orange peel, nutmeg and nuts.

Combine all ingredients and enjoy.

Charlie's Fancy Slow

Charles Norton

½ c. sugar
½ c. mayo
2 Tbsp. sour cream
¼ c. butter milk
¼ c. milk
1 Tbsp. vinegar
1 tsp. grated lemon peel
½ tsp. salt
½ tsp. celery seed
¼ c. caraway seed
⅛ tsp. ground black pepper
1 med. head cabbage (12 c.) shredded.
4 med. Carrots (2 c.) shredded.

Dressing in small bowl combine sugar, mayo, and sour cream, add milks vinegar, lemon peel, salt, celery seed, caraway seed and pepper, Wisk till smooth.

In lg. bowl combine cabbage and carrots. Pour dressing over cabbage and carrots, toss to coat.

Loria's Taco Salad

Loria Flynn

2 lbs. ground beef
½ head of lettuce
2 med. Tomatoes
1 sm. Onion
1 pkg. taco seasoning
1 can of refried beans
1 reg. bag of Doritos

Take ground beef brown it mixes with taco seasoning. cook as directed. Take Doritos put in lg. bowl put taco meat on it put beans on that cheese and lettuce and tomatoes. Taco sauce if like.

Cole Slaw
Loria Flynn

1 med. cabbage head
4 carrots
½ c. Mayo
2 Tbsp. Vinegar
2 Tbsp. Sugar

Shred cabbage and carrots mix mayo and sugar together with vinegar with vegetables refrigerate till ready to eat.

Potato Salad
Loria Flynn

4 c. potatoes boiled and chopped up.
4 eggs boiled and chopped up.
1 med. onion chopped.
⅔ c. celery
2 Tbsp. sweet relish
2 Tbsp. dill relish
¾ c. mayo
2 Tbsp. mustard
½ tsp. garlic
Salt pepper

Boil potatoes till tender enough to eat and boil eggs till done; chop both potatoes and eggs and onion and celery into lg. bowl then mix in rest of ingredients mix well and refrigerate till cool and serve.

Loria's Potatoes Salad for James Head

Loria Flynn

4 to 6 potatoes
4 eggs
⅔ c. celery
2 Tbsp. sweet relish
2 tbsp. dill relish
¾ c. mayo
2 Tbsp. mustard
Salt
Pepper
1 Tbsp. garlic

Boil potatoes till tender enough to eat, boil eggs till done, chop up to small pieces.

Mix all ingredients together chill and serve.

Pasta Salad

Loria Flynn

9 oz. tortellini

15 ½ oz. cheese tortellini

4 oz. parmesan cheese, grated.

1 (15 ½ oz.) can artichoke heart, drained, cut up

1 (6oz.) can pitted black olives, drained and cut up

16 oz. bottle of Italian dressing

1 pkg. hidden valley ranch dressing mix

1 (15 ½ oz.) can garbanzo beans, drained, and rinsed

1 med. red bell pepper, chopped.

1 med. red onion chopped.

1 head broccoli chopped into flowerets and blanched.

3 ripe avocadoes, chopped –if like

Mix the Italian dressing and the dry ranch dressing mix and set aside. Cook tortellini according to package instructions(aldonate)drain and rinse with warm water. Toss with olive oil, beans, red pepper, red onions. add dressing and mix well. Before serving add blanched broccoli toss and enjoy. if you want avocadoes and now and toss.

Cole Slaw

Linda Head-Driggers

head of cabbage
1 med. pack of carrots
Mayo
1 tsp. Vinegar
1 Tbsp. Sugar
Salt
Pepper

Shred cabbage and carets, add vinegar, sugar salt and pepper to taste, mix in mayo till all covered the way you like.

Mix well and enjoy. Serve cold.

Orange Jell-O salad

Margaret Ralls

12 oz. crushed pineapple (drained)
2 oz. orange Jell-O
12 oz. small curd cottage cheese
8 oz. mini marshmallows

Mix Jell-O as directed the add everything but cheese the let cool and set up. When sever on cottage cheese.

Chicken salad Bake

Margaret Ralls

c. chopped chicken.
2 ribs celery cleaned and chopped.
1 sm. Onion finely chopped.
1 jar (2 oz.) chopped pimientos.
1 can (10 ¾) cream of chicken soup
⅓ c. mayo
¾ c.(3oz.) shredded cheddar cheese
¾ c. crushed potato chips.

Preheat oven to 425★ in a lg. bowl mix chicken, celery, onion, pimientos, soup, and mayo; mix well and pour into an 8 in. square baking pan sprinkle with the cheese and potato chips. Bake 20 min. or until heated throw.

Chicken Salad

Margaret Ralls

2 ½ c. cooked chicken

1 c. chopped celery.

1c. green grapes, halved.

1 Tbsp. lemon juice

1 Tbsp. cider vinegar

1 ½ tsp. mustard

½ tsp. salt

½ tsp. sugar

⅛ tsp. black pepper

Toasted almonds

½ mayo

1 chopped apple

Mix everything well and enjoy.

Vegetable Salad

Margaret Ralls

1 can whole kernel corn drained.

1 can peas drained.

1 can French style green brans drained.

1 bell pepper chopped fine.

1 onion chopped fine.

1 sm. Jar pimento

1c. sugar

1c. vinegar

½ c. oil

½ tsp. salt

Mix well let set in frigerated 24 hrs.

Crunchy Pea Salad

Margaret Ralls

1 pkg. frozen peas
1 c. chopped cauliflower.
1 c. chopped.
1 c. slivered almonds
¼ c. green onions
1 c. ranched dressing
½ c. sour cream
½ tsp. dill weed.
¼ tsp. salt
⅛ tsp. pepper

Mix well and serve cold.

Waldorf Salad

Margaret Ralls

1c. fresh cauliflower
1 c. chopped celery.
1 apple cored but not peeled.
1 tsp. coconut extract
Dash of salt
2Tbsp. sugar
1Tbsp. mayo
1 Tbsp. lemon juice

Mix and chill.

Cabbage and Apple Slaw
Margaret Ralls

1lb. shredded cabbage (7c.)
¼ c. chopped red onion.
2 Granny Smith Apples
½ c. chopped walnuts.
¼ c. cider vinegar
¼ c. apple cider
1 ½ tsp. honey
1 Tbsp. finely chopped fresh parsley.

In lg. bowl combine first 4 ingredients. In sm. Bowl whisk together vinegar, cider and honey. Add salt and pepper to taste.

Toss dressing with vegetables. Sprinkle with parsley. Chill until ready to serve.

Chef Snack

Gwen Wilemon

2 c. multi-bran check
Butter spray
Worcestershire sauce
Garlic powder
2 c. Chex with
Sprinkle

Spray the 2 cups Chex with butter spray- sprinkle some Worcestershire sauce and garlic powder and back it for awhile at 350★

Mexican Dip

Gwen Wilemon

1 can refried beans.
Picante sauce
1 ½ c. avocado dip 12 oz.
1 pt. sour cream 16 oz.
1 purple onion
1 lg. tomato
10–12 oz. cheddar cheese grated.

Serve with chips.

Potato Salad
Loria Flynn

3 lbs. small red potatoes
3 hard -boiled eggs diced.
¼ c. sweet pickle juice
Salt
Pepper
Season salt
1 sm. Red onions finely chopped.
1 c. sour cream
1 c. mayo
1lg. green pepper, diced.
Paprika

Peel and halves
Peel and halve potatoes, boil in lg. saucepan until tender. Cool and cut into ½ in. or smaller pieces. Fold in remaining ingredients. all at once refrigerate before serving.

Cranberry Salad

Margaret Ralls

1 pkg. cranberries
2 c. sugar
2 c. water
1 c. marshmallows
2 sm. Pkg. Jell-O any flavor
1 can crushed pineapple with juice.
1 c. celery
1 c. nuts
1 c. apples

Cook cranberries with sugar and water cook until they pop. mix Jell-O any flavor.

As directed. Mix in pineapple let cool then add celery, nuts, apples and marshmallows.

Christy's Salad

Margaret Ralls

Good lettuce leaves
Grated carrots
Diced apples
Nuts
Raspberry dressing

Quick Cabbage Soup

1 c. frozen diced onion

½ c. frozen diced green bell pepper

3 stalks celery, diced.

1 Tbsp. minced garlic

2 boxes(32oz.) chicken broth

1 envelope(1oz.) dehydrated onion soup mix

2 bay leaves

½ tsp. ground black pepper

1 can (14.5) diced tomatoes.

1 bag (16 oz.) frozen mixed vegetables

1 bag. (16oz.) coleslaw blend

Cook till tender.

W.W. No Point Soup

Margaret Ralls

⅔ c. sliced carrots

½ c. diced onions

2 garlic cloves, minced.

3 c. broth (beef, chicken, or vegetable)

1 ½ c. diced green cabbage.

½ c. green beans

1 Tbsp. tomato paste

½ tsp. dried basil

¼ tsp. dried oregano

¼ tsp. salt

½ c. diced zucchini

Boils tell tender enough to eat.

Mexican Tortilla Soup
Loria Flynn

2 c. chopped tomatoes.
4 cloves garlic
1 sm. onion chopped up.
3 c. tortilla chips, divided.
2 Tbsp. corn oil
1 tsp. red pepper flakes
½ tsp. pimenton (smoky paprika)
4 c. chicken
2 (4oz.) boneless, skinless chicken Breast, cut into cubes
½ c. chopped cilantro.
1 avocado, peeled, cut into cubes.
¾ c. dairy sour cream
2 lg. limes, cut into wedges.

Place tomatoes, garlic, onion and 1 c. of the tortilla chips in food processor or blender; puree.

Heat oil in lg. heavy saucepan over low heat; add puree, simmering 15 to 20 min. or until flavors have blended and onion is cooked.

Add pepper flakes and pimenton, stirring to mix. Add chicken broth; bring to boiling over med. heat. Reduce heat; add chicken and simmer 10 min. more.

Serve soup in individual bowls topped with cilantro. Serve avocado sour cream and limes, if desired, on lg. platter with tortilla strips in small mounds or in individual bowls.

Beefy Green Chile Stew   Julia Flynn

2 lbs. boneless beef round steak, cut into bite-size pieces.
1 Tbsp. vegetable oil
2 lbs. red potatoes, cut into 1in. pieces
2 (14 ½) can beef broth
1 lg. onion, chopped.
2 (4oz.) cans diced green Chile peppers, drained
1 ½ tsp. minced fresh garlic
½ tsp. ground cumin
Flour tortillas, warmed (optional)

In 4-quart Dutch oven brown meat, half at a time, in hot oil over medium-high heat. Return all meat to pan. Stir in potatoes, diced tomatoes, broth, onion, Chile peppers, garlic, cumin and salt and ground black pepper to taste.

Bring to boiling; reduce heat to low. Cover and simmer 35 to 40 min. or until potatoes are tender.

Serve hot, ladled into bowls. Serve with warm flour tortillas, if desired.

Black Bean-Corn Soup

Julia Flynn

1 lb. Ground Beef
1 (1.25) pkg. taco seasoning
1 (1oz.) pkg. Ranch seasoning and salad dressing mix
½ tsp. ground cumin
1 (28 0z.) can diced tomatoes
1 (16 oz.) can black beans, rinsed and drained
1 (15 ¼ oz.) whole kernel corn, drained
1 (14 ½ oz.) can diced tomatoes with mild green chilies
2 c. water
½ c. shredded cheddar cheese

In 4 qt. Dutch oven cook ground beef until brown; drain fat. Add taco seasoning, salad dressing mix, cumin, tomatoes, black beans, corn, tomatoes with chilies, and water. Bring to boiling; reduce heat. Cover and simmer.

1 hr. top with cheddar cheese,

Vegetables & Side Dishes

Black Beans, Corn and Sausage Soup
Julia Flynn

1 lb. smoked sausage, sliced into ¼ in. pieces.
1 Tbsp. olive oil
1c. chopped onion
1 lg. clove garlic, minced.
1 tsp. chili powder
½ tsp. ground cumin
2 (14oz.) cans vegetables broth
1 (15oz.) can black beans, washed and drained
1 c. canned or frozen corn
¼ c. diced red pepper.
Tortilla chips, crushed.

In lg. saucepan, brown sausage in olive oil. Add onion, garlic, chili powder and cumin; cook 3 min. more. Add remaining ingredients.

Bring mixture to a boil; reduce heat and simmer 5 min. blend flyovers. Serve with tortilla chips.

Quick and Easy Noodle Soup

Loria Flynn

1 (32oz.) carton chicken broth
1 med. carrot peeled and diced.
1 med. rib celery halved lengthwise and sliced.
1 med. onion, cut into thin wedges.
1 tsp. dried marjoram
1 bay leaf
¼ tsp. pepper
2 c. chopped or shredded cooked meat (whatever you want)
½ c. uncooked med. egg noodles (about 1 ½ oz.)
2 Tbsp. chopped fresh parsley.
2 c. water

In Dutch oven or lg. saucepan, combine chicken broth, 2 c. water, carrot, celery, onion, marjoram, bay leaf and pepper. Bring to boiling. Reduce heat; cover and simmer 10 min.

Increase heat to med. high; return to boiling. Add turkey, noodles and parsley, if desired. Return to boiling. Reduce heat to med. cook, loosely covered, 15 to 20 min. or until noodles are tender. Remove and discard bay leaf.

Classic Chili

Loria Flynn

1 Tbsp. oil
1 ½ c. ground beef or turkey
½ c. chopped green pepper.
1 c. chopped onions.
½ c. chopped celery.
1 tsp. chopped fresh garlic.
3 cans (14.5 oz.) whole tomatoes, undrained
2 cans (15 oz.) kidney beans, undrained
2 Tbsp. chili powder
1 Tbsp. Worcestershire sauce
1 ½ tsp. dried oregano
1 ½ tsp. ground cumin
1 tsp. season salt
1 tsp. sugar
¼ tsp. pepper
¼ tsp. ground red pepper

Heat oil in Dutch oven over med. heat; brown ground beef and drain. Add green pepper, onion, celery and garlic, stirring occasionally.

Stir in all remaining ingredients. Continue cooking until mixture comes to a boil. Reduce to low heat through until flavors are blended, about 30 min.

Leek and Potato Soup

Loria Flynn

1 sticks butter
1 lg. onion, chopped.
2 leeks, chopped.
3 med. potatoes, peeled.
1 liter veg. stock
1 bay leaf
Sea salt and black pepper to taste

Sauté the onions in butter over a low heat for 5 min. cube the potatoes and add with the chopped leeks. Only use the lightest green parts of the leeks.

Add the vegetable stock and bay leaf and bring to a boil. Simmer until the vegetable are tender.

Remove the bay leaf, liquidize half the soup, then return it to the pan. Reheat and ladle into bowls.

Chili Mac Soup

Margaret Ralls

1 Lb. ground chuck
1 c. onion, chopped.
1can (16 oz.) hunts tomato sauce
4 c. tomato juice
1 (16 oz.) can red kidney beans
2 ½ c. water
4 tsp. chili seasoning
⅔ c. uncooked macaroni

Brown meat and onions add other ingredients bring to a boil. Cover and let simmer 15min.

W.W. Country French Vegetable Soup

Margaret Ralls

2 tsp. oil
2 c. green cabbage
1 c. chopped onion.
1 c. carrot
1 c. celery
1 c. potato
1 tsp. caraway seeds
1 c. water
2 (14oz.) veg. broth
1 c. white beans drained.
2 Tbsp. dried dill
½ tsp. pepper

Cook om med. heat till all is well blended and soft enough to eat.

Beans Soup

Margaret Ralls

8 oz. ground beef

2 c. fresh sliced mushrooms

1 c. beef broth

3 Tbsp. Bisquick mixed with broth (put in jar and shake) some parsley.

15oz. great northern beans

Black-Eyed Pea Soup

Loria Flynn

1 ½ c. dried, black-eyed peas
2 med. potatoes peeled and sliced.
3 celery stalks, sliced.
2 carrots, sliced.
1 med. onion, chopped.
2 cloves of garlic, chopped.
1 tsp. dried basil leaves
¼ tsp. pepper
3 Tbsp. soy sauce
2 Tbsp. chopped fresh dill weed.
More fresh dill weed if desired.

Rinse black eyed peas well. Place in 4 qt. pan; add potatoes, carrots, onion, garlic, basil and pepper with 7 1/7 c. water.

Bring to boiling. Reduce heat, cover and simmer 45 to 60 min. or until peas are tender. Stir in soy sauce and dill weed. Simmer 5 min. more. Season to taste with salt and pepper.

Mash peas and potatoes against sides of pan to thicken soup. Top each serving with additional fresh dill weed, if desired.

Frogman Stew

Margaret Ralls

5 qt. water
¼ c. bag (Crab or Shrimp Boil)
4 lbs. red potatoes
2 lbs. kielbasa or any smoke sausage cut into 1 ½ "pieces.
6 ears of corn
1 lemon
4 lbs. unpeeled shrimp

Can add a small head of cabbage cook shrimp 3 to 4 min. until it turns pink.

Cheeseburger Soup

Margaret Ralls

½ lb. ground beef
¾ c. onion chopped.
¾ c. shredded carrots
¾ c. celery
1 tsp. dried basil
1 tsp. parsley flakes
¾ tsp. salt
4 Tbsp. butter
3 c. chicken broth
4 c. diced potatoes
¼ c. flour
2 c. (8 oz.) American cheese
1 ½ c. milk
¼ c. sour cream

Brown beef sauté onion carrots basil and parsley in 1 Tbsp. of butter till tender. Add broth, potatoes and beef.

Bring to a boil reduce heat simmer about 12 min. with flour and butter make sauce till bubbly add to potatoes cook 5 min. add cheese milk salt pepper after cheese melts remove and fold in sour cream.

Slow – Cooked Harvest Beef and Veggies Stew   Grace Head

2 ½ lb. beef stew meat, cut into 1 ½ to 2 in." cubes.
½ tsp. salt
½ tsp. garlic pepper
3 c. baby carrots
1 lb. med. red potatoes, cut into 1 ½ to 2 in." pieces.
1 med. onion, cut into thin wedges.
1 (15 oz.) can diced tomatoes with green pepper, celery and onions
1 pkg. beefy-onion soup mix
2 tsp. dried marjoram
¼ c. flour (optional)
⅓ c. water or beef broth (optional)

Place beef in slow cooker, sprinkle with salt and garlic pepper; toss well. Add carrots, potatoes, onions, tomatoes, soup mix. Cover and cook 8 to 10 hrs. on low until beef is very tender.

If desired, thicken by blending ¼ c. flour into ⅓ c. water. Stir into beef mix. Cover. Cook on high 10 to 20 min. or until thickened.

Rutabaga and chicken stew
Loria Flynn Via Charles Norton

1 sm. Rutabaga, peeled and diced in ½ in." pieces.

2 med. parsnips, peeled and diced in ½ in." pieces.

1 med. carrot, peeled and diced in ½ in." pieces.

2 Tbsp. butter

1 lb. boneless, skinless chicken thighs, cut bite – size pieces.

⅓ c. flour

¼ tsp. salt

¼ tsp. pepper

1 lg. leek, chopped.

2 c. chicken broth

2 Tbsp. chopped fresh Italian parsley.

Bring lg. pot of lightly salted water to boiling. Add rutabaga, parsnips and carrots. Cover and cook 10 min. or until tender. Drain and set aside.

While veggies are cooking, melt butter in lg. pot over med. heat. Dust chicken with flour seasoned with salt and pepper, reserving any leftover flour. Brown chicken half at a time in pot with butter; remove chicken when brown. Add leek to pot. Sauté 3 min. or until tender. Add 1 Tbsp. reserved flour to pot. Stir to form paste. Stir in chicken broth. Bring to boiling, stirring frequently.

Return chicken to pot. Add veggies; reduce heat to low, cover and simmer 10 min. sprinkle with chopped parsley.

Classic Beef Stew

Loria Flynn

¼ c. flour
½ tsp. salt
¼ tsp. pepper
¼ tsp. garlic powder
2 lbs. beef stew meat trimmed if necessary.
1 lg. onion, chopped.
1 lb. baby carrots
1 stalk celery, chopped.
1 ½ lb. potatoes, peeled and cut up.
1 (14.5) can beef broth.
1 Tbsp. Worcestershire sauce
1 Tbsp. corn starch

Mix flour, salt, pepper and garlic powder in slow cooker. Add beef; stir to coat. Add onion, carrots, celery and potatoes, beef broth and Worcestershire sauce; stir.

Cover; cook on low 5 ½ to 7 ½ hours.

Mix cornstarch with 2 Tbsp. water. Stir into stew. Cover: cook 30 min. more or until carrots are cooked and meat is tender.

Collard Greens Soup
Grace Head

1 (14oz.) pkg. turkey sausage cut into ¼ in." slices
1 onion finely chopped.
1 green pepper seeded and chopped.
1 Tbsp. vegetable oil
2 (32 oz.) pkg. chicken broth
½ (16 oz.) pkg. fresh collard greens
1 (15.8 oz.) can black-eyed peas, rinsed and drained
¼ tsp. freshly ground pepper
Dash hot sauce

Sauté turkey sausage, onion, and green pepper in hot oil in Dutch oven over med. high heat 5 min. or until lightly browned.

Add chicken broth, collard greens, black-eyed peas, pepper, and hot sauce; bring to a boil. Cover, reduce heat, and simmer 30 min. stirring occasionally.

Cream of Leek Soup
Charles Norton

4 bacon strips, diced.
3 medium leeks (white portion only), sliced.
1 med. onion, chopped.
4 lg. potatoes peeled and sliced.
4 c. chicken broth
2 c. half- and- half cream
2 Tbsp. minced fresh parsley.
Salt to taste
pepper to taste

in a pressure cooker, cook bacon over med. heat until crisp. Remove with a slotted spoon to paper towels. In the drippings, sauté leeks and onions until tender. Add potatoes and broth. Close cover securely; place pressure regulator on vent pipe.

Bring cooker to full pressure over high heat. Reduce heat to med. high and cook for 5 min. (pressure regulator should maintain a slow steady rocking motion; adjust heat if needed)

Remove from the heat. Immediately cool according to manufacturer's directions until pressure is completely reduced. Uncover, cool soup slightly. In a blender, process soup in batches until smooth. Return all to the pan. Add cream and parsley; heat through over med. low heat (do not boil). Season with salt and pepper.

Garnish with bacon

VEGETABLES

Yellow Squash Casserole

Genie Thompson

¼ c. oleo
1 squash thickly sliced.
⅓ c. onion chopped.
1 Tbsp. pimento chopped.
1 Tbsp. sugar
½ c. shredded mild cheese.
½ c. mayo
½ tsp. salt
½ tsp. pepper

Pour melted oleo in 1 ½ qt. Casserole pan. add squash and sprinkle with salt and pepper.

Combine egg, mayo, green pepper, onion, pimento and sugar.

Mix well and pour over squash sprinkle evenly with cheese bake at 350 for 35 min.

Baked Egg

Carroll Ann Tolleson

1 Ex-large egg
A few chopped pecans
A few raisins
A little milk
Multigrain club crackers
Butter
Salt
Pepper

Butter a soufflé dish and break one egg in it leave whole, salt and pepper egg to taste, add raisins and chopped nuts on the top of egg. barely cover with milk.

(yellow may stick out a little). Now roughly crush crackers and top milk later, lastly dot with lightly salted butter on top of crackers. bake on a cookie sheet at 400 for 25 to 30 min. till as brown as you like it.

Funeral Corn

Margaret Ralls

1 bag of frozen corn
8 oz. cream cheese
1 stick butter
½ c. sugar

Mix and cook for 45 min. tell done.

Macaroni and Cheese

Ione Brown

1 -8oz bag macaroni
2 c. grated cheddar cheese
2 Tbsp. chopped onion.
1 egg beaten.
2 c. evaporated milk
1 tsp. salt
1 tsp. paprika
2 Tbsp. butter

Pre-heat oven to 375 grease a 2 qt. casserole dish. Cook and drain the macaroni and layer half of it in the casserole. Top with half the cheese and half the onion, repeat layers combine the egg evaporated milk and salt in a mixing bowl pour it over the macaroni sprinkle with paprika and dot with butter bake for 40 min. let it set 10 min. Before serving.

Louisiana Yummy

__1st layer_____-
1 stick butter melted.
1 c. flour
10 finely chopped pecans

__2nd. layer_____
1-8 oz. pkg. cream cheese
1 c. powder sugar
1 c. Kool whip

__3rd.layer_____
1-3oz.pkg. instant chocolate pudding
1-3 oz. pkg. instant vanilla pudding
3 c milk

__4th.layer_____
Kool-whip

1st. layer
Mix all together put in 9 x 12 pan and bake at 350 for 12 min.

2nd.layer
Beat until smooth, spread over cooled first layer.

3rd.layer
Mix all together and beat until thick pour over 2nd layer.

4th layer
Spread over 3rd.layer chopped pecans on top for decoration refrigerate.

Green Bean Casserole

Margaret Ralls

1 qt. green beans
1 can cream of mushroom soup.
1 lg. can French fried potatoes
1 lg. onion

Brown chopped onions add green beans and potatoes pour soup over the top bake 450 for 45 min.

Zucchini Casserole
Pat Hauser

4 c. squash chopped.
1 c. onion chopped.
¼ c. water
2 Tbsp. butter
½ tsp. salt
⅛ tsp. pepper
1 egg
1 c. cracker crumbs
3 Tbsp. butter

Combine squash and onions in saucepan, add water cover and cook until tender, drain well, mash squash. Cool add egg and mix thoroughly. Pour into grease baking dish. top with crumbs that have been browned in butter. Bake on 350 ovens for 30 min.

Quick Easy Egg Dish

Ione Brown

3 c. cooked macaroni
3 Tbsp. butter
2 lg. beaten eggs.

Put 3 c. macaroni and butter in a heavy skillet pour eggs into it and scramble.

Elegant Potatoes

Pat Houser

6 med. Potatoes
Season salt
Salt
Pepper
Parsley
Paprika
½ pt. whipping cream

Boil potatoes in skins then chill peel potatoes and grated layer potatoes in baking dish, sprinkle with season salt, salt, pepper, parsley, paprika continue to layer this way.

Before baking pour whipping cream on top bake covered in 325m oven for 1 ½ hour

Eggplant Parmesan Cheese

Beverly King

1 lg. eggplant
Salt
Pepper
1 c. breadcrumbs
2 lightly beaten eggs.
Vegetable oil
½ c. tomato sauce
½ lb. mozzarella cheese

Wash eggplant and cut in cross wise rounds ⅛ inch thick. Do not peel, season with salt and pepper Refrigerate cover with water for at least 2 hrs. dip in eggs, then breadcrumbs. Place in skillet containing ⅛ in, oil. Fry eggplant slices until tender and golden brown on both sides. Add oil when necessary, drain on paper towels. Line a shallow 2 qt. baking dish with some of the sauce arrange a layer of mozzarella slices more sauce and sprinkling of basil and parmesan cheese.

Repeat until eggplant in used. Bake at 350 for 25 to 30 min.

Pickled Carrots

Genie Thompson

5 c. sliced carrots 2 lbs.

1 med. Onion chopped.

1 sm. pepper chopped.

1 can tomato soup.

½ c. salad oil

1 c. sugar

1 tsp. salt

1 tsp. lea & Perrins

½ tsp. pepper

Cook carrots until tender drain and cool, mix other ingredients and pour over carrots. refrigerate for 12 hrs. will keep for 2 weeks.

Quick Quiche

Al Miller

1 can crescent rolls
Ham
bacon
zucchini
broccoli
shrimp or mushrooms
for main ingredients

pick main ingredient first and cook it first. Put about 1 c. of it in pie pan. Beat together 3 or 4 eggs add about ¼ c. canned milk or cream add salt and pepper to taste, pour into pie pan. place slices of mozzarella or Monterey jack cheese on top. Bake at 350 until sits.

Sweet Potatoes

Alberta Kennedy

6 lg. sweet potatoes
1 stick butter
1 c. brown sugar
Salt to taste
½ c. water
1 c. white sugar

Peel and slice potatoes arrange in 9 x 13 in. baking dish. Slice butter over potatoes sprinkle with brown and white sugar salt to taste add water.

Cover and bake 350 until tender.

Yellow Squash Casserole

Al Miller

2 lbs. yellow squash
½ lg. onion chopped.
1 sleeve Ritz crackers (about 35)
1 c. cheddar cheese grated.
2 eggs
¾ c. butter melted.
Salt
Pepper

Preheat oven to 400 lightly steam squash and onions in basket for 5 min. (or cook in microwave) drain and let set a said. crush crackers in to crumbs and combine with cheese (use med. bowl) put drained squash and onions in lg. bowl add ½ crackers and cheese mix to it in a sm. bowl mix to eggs and milk add to squash mixture, melt butter and add ½ to squash mix season with salt and pepper to taste spread squash mix. In 9 x 13 baking dish, top with reaming cracker mix then pour remaining butter over dish. bake in oven for about 25 min. until lightly brown.

Cream Corn

Teresa Murphy

1 lg. bag frozen corn
1-8 oz. cream cheese
1 stick of butter
Salt
Pepper

Put all ingredients in a crock pot turn on high stir occasionally add chopped green on.

Green Bean Casserole

Loria Flynn

3 pkg (9 oz.) frozen French style green beans
1 Tbsp. butter
1 Sm. Onion, chopped
1 pkg. (8 oz.) sliced mushrooms.
1 can (10 ¾ oz.) cream of mushroom soup
1 can (8oz.) sliced water chestnuts, drained.
¼ tsp. pepper
1 ½ c. shredded cheddar cheese
1 can (6 oz.) French fried onions

Cook green beans in microwave according to package directions. Place in lg. bowl; set a said.

Preheat oven to 375. Heat butter in lg. skillet oven med. heat. add onion and mushrooms, stirring about 5 min. or until tender; add to green beans. Stir in mushroom soup and next 3 ingredients, mixing well. spoon half of green beans mixture into lightly greased 1 ¾ qt. casserole; top with ½ of French-fried onions. Add remaining half of green bean mixture and top with remaining French-fried onions.

Bake uncovered 20 min.

Cauliflower with tomatoes and onions

Loria Flynn

1 (14 ½ oz.) can stewed tomatoes, cut up
½ c. onion, chopped.
1 clove garlic, minced.
4 c. cauliflower florets
3 Tbsp. fresh lemon juice
1 tsp. sugar
¼ tsp. ground black pepper
1 Tbsp. chopped fresh parsley.

In lg. saucepan combine undrained tomatoes, onion and garlic. Bring to boiling. Reduce heat, cover and simmer about 5 min. or until onion is tender.

Stir in cauliflower, lemon juice, sugar and pepper. bring to boiling. Reduce heat, cover, and simmer about 8 to 10 min. or until cauliflower is tender. Sprinkle with parsley before serving. Use slotted spoon to serve.

Seasoned Rice

Loria Flynn

2 Tbsp. olive oil
1 med. onion, diced.
½ each red and green bell pepper, seeded and diced.
1 sm. Tomato seeded and diced.
3 cloves garlic, minced.
6 oz. Spanish- style chorizo, sliced.
1 ½ c. long-grain rice

In deep skillet, heat olive oil over medium – high heat. add onion, peppers and tomatoes; cook until vegetable is tender. Add tomato paste, garlic and chorizo; stir to coat vegetables.

Add rice; stir to coat. add 2 cups water and bring to boiling; reduce heat to simmering. Cover and cook 20 min. taste for doneness; rice should be tender. Add more water, if necessary, and cook 5 min. more.

Remove rice from heat and season to taste with salt and pepper, fluff rice with fork and let stand, covered, 10 min. before serving.

Green Beans with Almonds

Charlie Norton

4 slices bacon, cut into small pieced.
6 c. fresh green beans trimmed and halved.
½ c. chopped onion.
1 clove garlic, minced.
¼ c. chopped red bell pepper.
¼ tsp. thyme leaves
¼ tsp. kosher salt
¼ tsp. ground black pepper
½ c. slivered almonds, toasted.

In med. skillet cook bacon pieces until crisp. Using slotted spoon, remove bacon from skillet, reserving drippings. Drain on paper towels.

Meanwhile, steam green beans over simmering water in steamer basket for 3 to 4 mins. Or until crisp tender. Cook onion and garlic in hot drippings in skillet until tender. Add green beans, bell pepper, thyme, salt and ground black pepper. Cook over low heat about 10 mins. Or until heated through. Stir in almonds sprinkle with bacon.

Okra

1 tsp. olive oil

¼ red onion, cut into thin wedges.

½ yellow bell pepper, seeded and cut into strips.

½ red bell pepper, seeded and cut into strips.

1 clove garlic, mined.

1 lb. fresh okra, trimmed and sliced into 1 in. pieces.

1 ½ tsp. fresh thyme

⅓ c. chicken broth

Preheat grill to med. place cast iron skillet on grill rack, heat oil in skillet. Add onion, bell pepper strips and garlic; cook and stir 1 min. add okra, thyme and broth; toss lightly to mix.

Heat until broth is steaming. Cover and cook over med. heat 10 min. season with and pepper to taste.

Brussels Sprouts and Walnuts   Loria Flynn

1 lb. sm. To med. brussels sprouts, bottoms trimmed.
1 ½ Tbsp. olive oil
1 tsp. balsamic vinegar
½ c. chopped walnuts.

Preheat oven to 375★ bring lg. pot of lightly salted water to boiling. add brussels sprouts. Cook 5 mins. Drain well and return to pot. Stir in olive oil and vinegar; season to taste with salt and pepper. Spread brussels sprouts in shallow lightly greased roasting pan. Bake 20 mins. Stirring once. Remove from oven, sprinkle walnuts over sprouts and roast 5 more mins.

Braised Vegetables

Loria Flynn

4 stalks celery, chopped.
8 oz. baby carrots
2 tsp. olive oil
2 granny smith apples cored and chopped.
1 c. golden raisins
¾ Tbsp. Dijon- style mustard

Cook celery and carrots in olive oil over med. heat 8 to 10 min. or until vegetables are crisp tender.

Add apples, raisins, apple juice, honey and mustard; stir well. Cover reduce heat to med. and cook 10 min. uncover and cook until liquid is absorbed, and vegetables are glazed.

Veggie Casserole
Loria Flynn

5 c. chopped broccoli.

1 ½ c. chopped yellow squash.

1 sm. Red onion, chopped.

2 carrots peeled and chopped.

2 Tbsp. olive oil

1 c. mayo

1 c. shredded cheddar cheese, divided.

½ c. fine dry breadcrumbs

¼ tsp. paprika

½ tsp. salt

¼ tsp. ground black pepper

Preheat oven to 325★ in lg. skillet, cook broccoli, squash, onion and carrots in oil over med. heat 5 to 7 mins. Or until crisp-tender. In sm. Bowl, stir together mayo. And ½ c. of cheese; stir into vegs. turn vegs. mixture into lightly greased 2 qts. Casserole dish.

In small bowl, stir together breadcrumbs, paprika, salt, pepper and remaining ½ c. cheese; sprinkle over vegs. Bake 20 to 30 min. or until light brown.

WW Confetti Cheese Omelet   Margaret Ralls

¼ c. red bell pepper
¼ c. green bell pepper
¼ c. chopped onions.
1 c. egg
salt
pepper
½ c. reduced fat cheddar cheese

Spray nonstick skillet add pepper and onions cook 4 min. or till tender.

Pour eggs in skillet – cook without stirring 2 to 3 min. until golden brown on bottom – sprinkle with cheese loosen omelet with spatula – fold in half cook 2 min. until egg is set and cheese is set and begins to melt. Cut omelet in half.

Sugar Snap Pea Succotash
Loria Flynn

1 pkg. (10oz.) fresh snap peas
1 can (14 oz.) corn, drained
½ c. sliced cherry tomatoes
6 green onions sliced and divided.
3 Tbsp. butter, cubed.
1 Tbsp. chopped fresh parsley.

Pre-heat grill to high. Place sugar snap peas, corn, tomatoes, half the green onions, and butter in lg. bowl; toss to combine. Season with salt and pepper to taste. Transfer sugar snaps mixture to a 9 x 13 in. piece of heavy – duty. aluminum foil. Fold up edges and crimp lightly to seal.

Grill foil packet 15 min. or until sugar snaps are tender. Carefully remove sugar snaps mixture from foil to serving bowl. Top with chopped parsley.

Hash Brown Casserole

Margaret Ralls

1 pkg.(32oz.) shredded frozen potatoes.
½ c. melted butter.
1 can cream of chicken soup.
1 pkg. (12oz.) grated American cheese.
1 tsp. salt
½ sm. Onion, chopped.
2 c. crushed corn flakes
½ c. melted butter.

Place thawed potatoes in a 9 x 13 baking dish mix together next 6 ingredients and pour drizzles melted butter over all bake uncovered at 350 ★ 45 min.

Vegetable Potpie

Loria Flynn

Pie Filling:
3 med. parsnips, peeled and diced in ½ in. pieces.
3 med. carrots, peeled and diced in ½ in. pieces.
1 med. sweet potato, peeled.
3 Tbsp. unsalted butter
2 c. sliced mushrooms
1 c. chopped leeks.
3 Tbsp. flour
2 c. veg. or chicken broth
⅛ tsp. dried thyme
¼ tsp. hot red pepper sauce
Drop biscuits:
2 ¼ c. prepared biscuit mix
¾ c. milk

Pre- heat oven to 400* to prepare filling, bring lg. pot of lightly salted water to boiling. Add parsnips, carrots and sweet potato.

Meanwhile, melt butter in lg. skillet over med. heat. add mushrooms wand leeks. Sauté 5 min. or until tender

Stir in flour. Gradually stir in broth. Add thyme, salt and pepper to taste and hot pepper. Stir in drained veg. spoon into 10 in. baking dish.

To prepare biscuit topping, combine biscuit mix and milk. Drop heaping tablespoons of batter onto veg. filling to form crust. Do not completely cover filling. Bake 18 to 20 mins. Or until biscuits are golden brown.

Brussels sprouts with Lemon
Loria Flynn

1 lb. fresh brussels sprouts, trimmed.
2 tsp. olive oil
½ sm. Onion, halved and thinly sliced.
1 tsp. grated lemon peel
2 tsp. fresh lemon juice
¼ tsp. pepper
⅛ tsp. salt

Trim outer leaves from brussels sprouts. With sharp knife, cut a small x in stems of sprouts; set aside.

Combine oil and onion in microwave- safe 1 qt. casserole; toss to coat onions. Microwave, covered, 1 min. add brussels sprouts and 3 Tbsp. water. Cover and microwave on high 6 to 9 mins. Or until brussels sprouts is crisp- tender, stirring once. Add lemon peel, pepper, and salt, if desired; toss to coat.

Spinach Pie

Loria Flynn

2 Tbsp. butter
3 Tbsp. flour
1 c. hot milk
¼ tsp. grated nutmeg
2 lbs. fresh spinach, cooked, well drained and chopped.
2 eggs, beaten.
4 bacon strips, cooked to crisp and crumbled.
2 eggs, hard boiled, sliced.
½ lb. queso, crumbled.
½ c. toasted breadcrumbs

Preheat oven to 375★ to prepare white sauce, melted butter in saucepan, add flour and stir. Gradually add milk, whisking constantly until thick. Add nutmeg and salt and pepper to taste. Set aside.

Place cooled spinach in lg. bowl, stir in beaten eggs, and white sauce; mix well. Butter 8 x 8 baking dish; and half of spinach mixture, top with crumbled bacon, hard – boiled eggs slices and cheese. Cover with remaining spinach mixture, top with breadcrumbs. Bake 25 min. until spinach mixture is firm to touch and golden. Allow to cool 30 before slicing.

Triple Cheese Pizza

Loria Flynn

½ c. ricotta cheese
¼ c. grated Parmesan cheese
1 egg white
2 Tbsp. freshly chopped parsley
1 (7 in.) pizza crust
2 Roma tomatoes thinly sliced.
1 clove garlic, minced.
2 Tbsp. chopped fresh basil.
¼ c. shredded mozzarella cheese
Crushed red pepper flakes.

Preheat oven to 450★ combine ricotta cheese, parmesan cheese, egg white and parsley in med. bowl. Spread mixture over pizza crust. Top tomatoes, garlic, basil and mozzarella cheese. Bake 8 to 10 min. or until thoroughly heated through and cheese is melted. Sprinkle with crushed red pepper flakes.

Season — Grilled Snow Peas
Loria Flynn

¼ c. rice wine vinegar
2 tsp. sesame oil
2 tsp. soy sauce
1 Tbsp. sugar
1 clove garlic, minced.
1 tsp. grated gingerroot
1lb. snow peas
2 tsp. sesame seeds, toasted.

Whisk together first 6 ingredients in a small bowl until blended. Place snow peas in a foil packet. Pour rice wine vinegar mixture over snow peas, seal packet. Grill over medium heat 7 to 10 min. or until tender. Sprinkle with toasted sesame seeds before serving. Serve immediately.

Tomato Ratatouille   Charlie Norton

1 med. eggplant peeled and diced.
2 med. zucchinis, sliced.
2 bell peppers seeded and sliced.
3 yellow onions peeled and diced.
6 cloves garlic, peeled.
1 c. sun dried tomatoes (not packed in oil)
1 c. chicken broth
Salt
pepper
3 sprigs fresh basil, chopped.

Place eggplant cubes in a lg. bowl of water. With scissors, cut dried tomatoes in half. Drain eggplant. Steam all vegetables with garlic until peppers are tender. Heat chicken broth in a pan until hot, and simmer vegetables about 3 min. salt and pepper vegetables to taste. Top vegetables with fresh basil.

Stuffed Mushrooms

Loria Flynn

50 sm. Mushrooms suitable for stuffing
½ c. camembert or brie, diced (including rind)
1 Tbsp. butter, softened.
1 c. walnut pieces finely chopped.
1 clove garlic, minced.
1 c. soft breadcrumbs
2 Tbsp. fresh parsley, chopped.
2 to 4 Tbsp. milk

Preheat oven to 400★ trim the stems off the mushrooms level with the gills. Chop stems and place in bowl.

Add cheese, butter, walnuts, garlic, breadcrumbs, parsley and enough milk to moisten. Mix well.

Place mushrooms (stem side up) in a lg. shallow, oven-proof dish. Put a spoonful of the mixture on top of each mushroom. Bake for 8 to 10 min. or until just tender.

Oven Roasted Squash

Loria Flynn

2 Tbsp. olive oil
2 to 3 Tbsp. Pepper
1 Tbsp. dried rosemary
1 lb. sm. Red potatoes, scrubbed, but into ½ in. dice.
1 ¼ lb. squash: zucchini, yellow summer and /or crookneck (use a combination if possible) in 1 in. dice.
1 lg. red onion, cut into 1 in. chunks.

Put oil, lemon pepper, rosemary (crush first) and potatoes into plastic bag. Shake well to coat. Add squash to bag; shake again to coat. Spread vegetables on shallow baking pan. Roast at 400 degrees, stir vegetables, and continue roasting until brown, about 20 min.

Cream Corn

Loria Flynn

1 lb. bag frozen corn
1 pkg.(8oz) cream cheese
1 stick butter
pepper

put all ingredients in a crock pot turn on high stir occasionally add chopped green onions.

Funeral Corn

Margaret Ralls

1 Bag of frozen corn
8 oz. cream cheese
1 stick butter
½ c. sugar

Mix and cook for 45 min. tell done.

Annatto-Spice Potato Cakes
Loria Flynn

3 lg. baking potatoes
1 tsp. annatto powder
6 green onions, finely minced
¼ lb. queso banco, coarsely grated.
Oil for frying
½ c. all-purpose flour
salsa

preheat oven to 375★ wash and dry potatoes, place potatoes in ovenproof dish and brush with oil. Bake uncovered 40 min; prick potatoes with fork and bake 20 min. more or until potatoes are soft, remove and cool.

Peel potatoes and mash in lg. bowl add annatto powder, green onions and queso Blanco; mix well. Using a tsp. form into balls. Refrigerate until completely cold.

Heat half in" of oil in nonstick skillet over med.- high heat. flatten potato balls into patties, lightly dust patties with flour on both sides and fry until golden brown on each side Drain on paper towels and season with salt and pepper to taste. Serve immediately with salsa.

Bake Yams in Orange Sauce

Loria Flynn

3 lg. Sweet potatoes cut lengthwise.
¾ c. orange juice
¾ c. brown sugar
½ tsp. ginger
½ tsp. salt
1 Tbsp. butter

Mix juice and other ingredients together and pour over potatoes and bake uncovered 350★ for 45 min. till tender enough to eat with turning occasionally.

Roasted Garlic Collard Greens

Loria Flynn

2 lbs. collard greens washed and chopped.
1(32 oz.) container chicken broth
4 lg. or 6 med. potatoes
1 whole bulb garlic
6 slices bacon
2 Tbsp. olive oil
3 Tbsp. butter

Preheat grill to med-high 350-400 combine broth and ½ c. water in lg. pot. Bring to boil. add collard greens. Return to boiling; reduce heat and simmer 45 mins. Drain and squeeze out excess water out. Set aside.

Meanwhile, wrap potatoes and garlic individually in aluminum foil. grill potatoes and garlic until fork-tender, about 45 min. to 1 hr. cool potatoes slightly and chop into lg. chunks. remove garlic cloves from bulb. set aside.

Place lg. cast iron skillet on grill rack. heat 3 min. add bacon to skillet on grill until crisp. Remove to cool, break into pieces. Drain excess drippings. Add oil and butter. add potatoes and garlic cloves. Cook and stir 5 min. stir in collard greens add crumbled bacon, and season with salt and pepper to taste. Cook 5 min. more.

Cooked Kale

Loria Flynn

2 bunches kale trimmed and chopped.
1 tsp. vegetable oil
2 cloves garlic, minced.
¼ tsp. cayenne pepper
2 tsp. toasted sesame oil
2 tsp. sesame seeds, toasted.

Bring 1 c. water to boiling in Dutch oven.

Add kale, cover and cook 4 min., stirring occasionally. Uncover and cook until water evaporates, about 3 mins. Heat veg. oil in heavy skillet over med. heat. sauté garlic and cayenne 1 min. add kale, cook and stir 3 mins. Transfer kale to bowl. Toss with sesame oil. Salt and pepper to taste. Garnish with sesame seeds.

Hash Brown Casserole

Loria Flynn

1 c. thinly sliced green onions.
1 c. (4 oz.) shredded reduced – fat sharp cheddar cheese (12 oz.) American cheese.
2 Tbsp. stick margarine, melted.
¼ tsp. pepper
1 pkg. (32 oz.) frozen Southern - style hash brown potatoes, thawed.
1 (8oz.) carton sour cream
1 can (10 ¾ oz.) condensed cream of mushroom soup, undiluted
Cooking spray
½ tsp. paprika

Preheat oven to 350★ combine first 7 ingredients in a lg. bowl and stir well. Spoon mixture into a 13 x 9 in" baking dish coated with cooking spray. Sprinkle paprika evenly over casserole. Bake at 350 for 1 hr. or until bubbly.

Pizza Spaghetti Bake   Margaret Ralls

1 chopped onions
1 pkg.(4oz.) sliced pepperoni.
⅓ c. butter melted.
6 oz. spaghetti
1 c. grated swiss cheese
1 lb. mozzarella cheese sliced.
2 cans(8oz.) tomato sauce
½ tsp. oregano
½ tsp. basil
1 can (4oz.) mushrooms drained (if desired)

Sauté onion in ½ of the butter preheat oven to 350★ pour butter in 11x7x2 baking dish toss cooked spaghetti in butter and onions cover spaghetti with one can of tomato sauce then add in order ½ of swiss cheese ½ of pepperoni ½ mozzarella cheese all mushrooms sprinkle with oregano and basil add more tomato sauce top with remaining swiss, pepperoni and mozzarella bake 350 for 20-25 mins.

WW Cheesy Bean Casserole

Margaret Ralls

1 c. chopped onion.
2 (15oz.) brown or chili beans drained
2 (14oz) chopped tomatoes
½ tsp. garlic powder
salt
pepper
4 oz. cheddar cheese
Water as needed.

Heat skillet, cook onions in butter the add the tomatoes and beans and seasonings to mix and let cook with water until beans and seasonings are mixed well and all the taste are mixed well.

Marinated Vegetable

Margaret Ralls

Broccoli
½ head of cauliflower
4 carrots sliced.
2 stalks celery
1 green bell pepper
3 oz. jar pimentos
¾ c. white or red vinegar
1 c. olive oil
¼ c. water
2 Tbsp. sugar
½ tsp. oregano

Mix ¾ c. white or red vinegar, oil, sugar, oregano and put in sm. Pot boil. let cool and then pour over the veggies.

Cheese -Filled Eggplant Rolls
Amira Flynn

1 lg. eggplant
2 Tbsp. Olive oil
½ tsp. kosher salt
½ tsp. ground pepper
⅓ c. ricotta cheese
⅓ c. goat cheese
1 ½ c. marinara sauce
½ c. shredded.
Hot cooked pasta

Preheat oven to 450★, line baking sheet with cooling rack.

Prepare eggplant by first cutting off stem and removing skin. Then slice length wise into slices about ¼ in. thick. Lay on prepared baking rack, brush with olive oil and seasoning with salt and pepper. Roast 8 to 10 min. or till done; cover with foil.

Combine ricotta cheese and goat cheese in small bowl.

Coat 8 x 8 in. baking dish with nonstick cooking spray. Assemble by spooning ¾ c. of the marinara sauce in baking dish. Spread 2 Tbsp. cheese mixture on each eggplant slice, roll, then place them seam-side down in prepared baking dish. Top rolls with remaining ¾ c. sauce and sprinkle with mozzarella cheese.

Bake 15 min. or until cheese is melted and lightly browned. Serve sauce and eggplant rolls over hot cooked pasta, id desired.

Thai Curry Stir Fry

Julia Flynn

1 c. chicken broth
1 Tbsp. soy sauce
2 tsp. cornstarch
2 tsp. curry powder
¼ tsp. red pepper
1 lb. boneless pork loin chops
½ med. onion, cut into slivers.
2 cloves garlic, minced.
3 c. broccoli flowerets
1 c. diagonally sliced carrot
1 tsp. canola oil
3 c. hot rice cooked.
¼ c. dry roasted peanuts

Stir together broth, soy sauce, cornstarch, curry powder, and red pepper. set aside.

Trim fat from pork chops. Thinly slice across the grain into bite-size strips. Set aside.

Lightly coat a nonstick wok or lg. skillet with cooking spray. Heat over med.-high heat; stir-fry onion and garlic for 1 min. remove from wok.

Add broccoli and carrots to wok. Stir broth mixture stir- fry for 2 to 3 min. or until crisp-tender. Remove from wok.

Add oil to wok. Stir -fry pork, half at a time, for 1 to 3 min. or until no longer pink. Return all pork to wok. Stir broth mixture and add to wok; cook and stir until broth is boiling and slightly thickened. Return all vegetables to wok and heat through.

Serve pork mixture over hot cooked rice. Sprinkle with peanuts.

Zucchini Frittata

Charlie Norton

2 lbs. zucchini
1 Tbsp. salt
¾ c. egg, lightly beaten.
1 sm. onion finely chopped.
1 tsp. dried oregano
1 tsp. dried basil
½ tsp. hot pepper flakes

1 ¾ c. (7 oz.) shredded Monterey jack cheese Trim ends from zucchini. Shred zucchini and place in colander set over a bowl. Add salt; toss to mix. Let stand 30 mins.

Press zucchini with back of spoon to squeeze out any excess moisture.

Preheat oven to 325★

Combine egg, onion, oregano, basil and hot pepper flakes. Stir in cheese and zucchini. Mix well pour mixture into greased 9 in. plate.

Bake 25 to 30 mins. Or until golden and set. Serve immediately or cool and serve at room temperature.

Greens and Citrus and Vinaigrette   Charlie Norton

⅓ c. fresh tangerine juice
2 Tbsp. balsamic vinegar
2 Tbsp. honey
1 clove garlic, minced.
½ tsp. salt
½ tsp. ground pepper
½ c. olive oil
6 c. mixed salad greens
2 sm. Tangerines, peeled, seeded and sectioned.
½ sm. Red onion, sliced.
¼ c. toasted almonds or pecans
4 sliced prosciutto

For dressing, blend tangerine juice, balsamic vinegar, honey, garlic, salt and pepper until smooth. With blender running, add olive oil in slow, steady stream until combined.

Divide greens among 6 salad plates. Arrange tangerine sections and onion slices on greens. Top with almonds and drizzle with dressing. Top evenly with evenly with prosciutto, if desired.

Honey Carrots

Loria Flynn

1 lb. medium carrots, peeled, or 1 lb. baby carrots.
1 Tbsp. honey
1 tsp. butter
¼ tsp. nutmeg or coriander

Cut med. carrots in half lengthwise. And then crosswise into 2 in. pieces. Or, cut baby carrots in half lengthwise. In lg. skillet, cook carrots, covered, in sm. Amount of boiling water 8 to 10 mins. Or until crisp-tender. Drain.

Add 2 Tbsp. water, honey, butter and nutmeg to skillet. Stir to combine. Bring to gentle boil and cook about 2 mins. More, stirring often, until carrots are glazed. Season to taste with salt.

Broccoli Medley

Loria Flynn

1 Tbsp. olive
1 Tbsp. olive oil
1 clove garlic, minced.
1 ¼ lb. broccoli, cut in bite-size pieces (5 c.)
½ red bell pepper, cut in thin strips.
½ yellow bell pepper, cut in thin strips.
2 Tbsp. soy sauce

Heat olive oil and garlic in wok or skillet. Add broccoli and stir-fry 1 min.

Add peppers and continue to stir-fry 3 to 4 mins. More or until vegetables are crisp-tender. Add soy sauce; cook and stir until heated through.

Grilled Chile Peppers

4 Anaheim chilies halved and seeded.
2 poblano chilies, halved and seeded.
2 Jalapeno chilies halved and seeded.
2 tsp. Vegetable oil
½ tsp. ancho or plain chili powder
½ tsp. ground cumin
¼ tsp. dried oregano
1 lg. clove garlic, minced (optional)

Heat grill to med. direct heat. meanwhile, prepare chilies.

Blend remaining ingredients in med. bowl. Add peppers; toss to coat. Place peppers on grill. Grill, covered, 7 to 12 min. or until tender- crisp and charred, turning once. Remove from grill. Coarsely chop peppers. Place in med. bowl with any accumulated juices; toss to mix.

Season with salt and pepper to taste. Serve in warm tortillas with grilled beef, pork, or chicken, or as an accompaniment to burgers, steaks, or chops.

Chevre and Onion Focaccia

Loria Flynn

1 loaf (1 lb.) bread dough, thawed according to package directions.
1 Tbsp. olive oil
1 med. red onion thinly sliced.
¼ tsp. black pepper
¼ tsp. crushed dried oregano
¼ tsp. crushed red pepper flacks
1 med. tomato cored and chopped.
1 Tbsp. capers
2 Tbsp. sliced ripe olives.
1 c. crumbled chevre cheese

Preheat oven to 400* roll out dough to 8 x 12 rectangle Place on greased baking sheet.

Heat oil in medium skillet over med. high heat. add onion, pepper, oregano and red pepper flakes; cook and stir 5 min. spread onion mixture over bread dough.

Sprinkle on chopped tomato, capers, olives and cheese.

Bake 15 to 18 mins. Or until bread is puffed and golden.

Eggplant Roll-up

Charlie Norton

1 ¼ c. bottled vinaigrette dressing
2 tsp. lemon pepper
1 tsp. dried basil, divided.
1 lg. eggplant peeled and sliced lengthwise into ½ in. thick slices.
½ c. chopped roasted red pepper.
¼ c. cream cheese, softened (4 oz.)
¼ c. feta cheese
1 clove garlic, minced.
¼ tsp. dried thyme

Combine vinaigrette, ¼ c. water, lemon pepper and ¾ tsp. of the basil in lg. Ziplock bag. Add eggplant; seal bag and toss to coat. Chill 1 hr.

Coat grill rack with nonstick cooking spray. preheat grill to med. direct heat. meanwhile, combine red pepper, cream cheese, feta, garlic, thyme and remaining ¼ tsp. basil in sm. Bowl; mix well. Chill

Remove eggplant from marinade. Grill 3 min. per side, or until eggplant is tender. Cool slightly.

Spoon about 2 Tbsp. feta mixture onto narrow end of each eggplant slice; roll up jelly-roll style. Cut roll into 1 ½ in. slices, secure with toothpicks. Top with additional red pepper strips, if desired. Serve warm or at room temperature.

Layered Cucumber Dip
Loria Flynn

1 pkg. (8oz.) cream cheese, softened.
2 Tbsp. milk
1 tsp. dried oregano leaves
¼ tsp. pepper
1 (8 oz.) container hummus
¾ c. chopped cucumber.
1 plum tomato, chopped.
½ c. (2oz) feta cheese
¼ c. sliced black olives.
2 Tbsp. sliced green onion.

Purchased pita crisps or assorted crackers.

In sm. Bowl stir together cream cheese, milk, oregano and pepper.

Spread cream cheese mixture on a 10 in. serving platter. Gently spread hummus on top. Sprinkle with cucumber, tomato, feta cheese, olives and green onions.

Cover and refrigerate at least 1 hr. serve with pita crisps or crackers.

Asadero Cheese and Bean Nachos

Loria Flynn

1 Tbsp. vegetable oil
1 sm. Onion finely chopped.
1 Chile pepper, cored, seeded, and minced.
1 can (15.25 oz.) black beans and well drained
¼ tsp. ground cumin
20 lg. tortilla chips
1 ¼ c. shredded asadero cheese, divided.

Preheat oven to 375★

Heat oil in skillet over med. heat. add onion and Chile; sauté 2 to 3 mins. Add beans. Heat over low heat while mashing with fork. Stir in cumin, and salt and pepper to taste.

Spread 1 Tbsp. bean mixture over each tortilla chip. Arrange on baking sheet. Sprinkle 1 Tbsp. cheese over each nacho. Bake 10 min. or until cheese melts.

Baked Beans

Linda Head - Driggers

2 cans navy beans
2 qts. Water (8 c.)
½ lb. salt park
2 Tbsp. brown sugar
½ tsp. dry mustard
1 sm. onion, chopped.
½ c. molasses
¼ c. catsup
¼ c. chili sauce

In lg. saucepan, cover beans with water. Soak overnight or about 12 hrs.

Heat beans and soaking water to boiling. Simmer covered, about 1 hr. or until beans are almost tender. Drain, reserve liquid. Heat oven to 300★. In bean pot or lg. casserole, combine beans and salt park. Add enough water to reserved beans liquid to measure 2 c. stir remaining ingredients into 2 c. liquid. Pour over beans, mix gently. Bake covered at 300★ for 6 to 7 hrs. stirring occasionally, adding water if necessary. Remove cover during last hr. of baking.

Refried Beans

Loria Flynn

2 to 4 Tbsp. oil, bacon drippings
2 c. cooked beans
¼ c. chopped green chilies if desired.
¼ c. chopped onions if desired.

In med. skillet, heat oil. Add beans and mash with potato masher or liquid evaporates and beans are of desired consistency, stirring occasionally. Stir in chilies.

Green Bean Casserole

Margaret Ralls

2 cans green beans drained.
1 can cream of mushroom soup (undiluted)
1 can French fried onions

Mix 2 cans of green beans(drained),1 can cream of mushroom soup undiluted bake 1 hr. at 350 the last 15 min. sprinkle top with ½ can French fried onions.

Sweet Potato Casserole

Loria Flynn

3 c. mashed sweet potatoes.
1 c. sugar
½ stick melted butter.
½ c. milk1 tsp. salt
2 eggs beaten.
1 tsp. vanilla
1 c. brown sugar
⅓ c. flour
⅓ stick butter
1 c. pecans (if desired)

Mix until fluffy pour in casserole dish. Mix sugar and butter and flour pour on top. And bake at 350 for 45 min. add marsh mellow to top if desired.

Sweet Potato Casserole

Loria Flynn

Beat 2 eggs in mixer.
1 c. sugar
1 tsp. vanilla
½ c. milk
¾ stick butter melted.
3 c. cooked, mashed sweet potatoes.

Topping:
1 c. brown sugar
⅓ c. flour
¼ stick oleo.
½ or 1 c. pecans

Mix until looks like meal with pastry blender. Spread on top of sweet potatoes; add chopped pecans, mixed in. Pat down and bake 45 mins. At 350★

Rice Pilaf
Loria Flynn

1 can (10 ½ oz.) beef broth

1 can (4 oz.) sliced mushrooms drained.

½ c. raw converted rice

2 Tbsp. butter

⅓ c. onion finely chopped.

Put all together in slow cooker cover and cook on low for 6 to 8 hrs.

Rosemary Potatoes

Charlie Norton

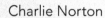

4 lbs. sm. red potatoes chopped.
⅓ c. olive oil
4 garlic cloves chopped.
1 c. chopped onion.
2 Tbsp. fresh rosemary chopped.
Salt
pepper

cut and clean vegies in lg. bowl mix all ingredients together put on cookie sheet bake till done.

Cole cannon

Charlie Norton

6 med. potatoes
1 onion chopped, finely.
2 c. cabbage chopped, finely.
1 Tbsp. butter
salt
pepper

put everything in pot and cook it all tell tender and mashed with butter
salt and pepper to taste.

Glazed Sweet Potatoes

Loria Flynn

4 med. sweet potatoes
¼ c. firmly packed brown sugar
¼ tsp. salt
¼ c. butter

Heat oven to 350★ peel cooked potatoes; cut into quarters or slice.

Arrange in shallow baking dish combine remaining ingredients. Drizzle over potatoes. Bake uncovered at 350★ for 20 to 30 mins.

Hash Brown Casserole

Loria Flynn

2 lbs. frozen hash browns
1 can cream of chicken soup.
2 c. American or cheddar cheese
1 stick butter
1 pt. sour cream
½ c. chopped onion.

Mix and put in casserole dish. Melt ¼ c. butter and pour over 2 c. crushed corn flakes. Sprinkle on top. Bake at 350★ for 45 to 50 mins.

Potatoes Cakes
Loria Flynn

Peeled potatoes, cooked and mashed 2 c.
1 egg
1 Tbsp. flour
2 Tbsp. whole milk
¼ c. veg. oil

Mix mashed potatoes, egg, flour and milk thoroughly.

Shape into flat cakes, about ½ inch. Thick.

Heat oil in skillet. Add potatoes cakes to hot skillet cook until golden brown and thoroughly heated.

Roasted Rosemary Potatoes

Loria Flynn

4 lbs. sm. variety potatoes
⅓ c. olive oil
3 to 4 cloves garlic, chopped.
1 c. chopped onion.
2 Tbsp. chopped fresh rosemary.
salt
pepper

heat oven to 425★ place potatoes, oil, garlic, onion, rosemary, and salt
and pepper in a lg. bowl. Toss well to mix. Spread onto by baking pan.
Bake 40 to 45 min. stirring occasionally, until potatoes are fork tender.

Red Beans and Rice

Loria Flynn

1 lb. dry beans
1 med. onion chopped.
1 sm. green pepper, chopped.
2 ribs celery, chopped.
3 cloves garlic, chopped.
2 cans (14 ½ oz.) beef broth
2 c. water
1 lb. smoked ham chopped.
1 tsp. salt
½ tsp. cumin
½ tsp. tabasco pepper sauce
3-4 c. rice cooked.

In a lg. pot, cover beans with 3 times their volume of water and bring to a boil.

Boil for 10 min. remove from heat. cover and let stand for 1 hr. drain beans combine all ingredients except rice in a slow cooker. Cover and cook on low for 10 – 12 hrs. on high 5-6 hrs. serve over rice.

Oven rice Pilaf

4 ½ c. water
2 Tbsp. butter
2 Tbsp. chicken bouillon
1 tsp. crushed thyme
2 c. long grain wild rice
2 c. shredded carrots
½ c. sliced green onion.
¼ c. onion
¼ c. parsley, chopped.

In med. saucepan, stir together first 4 ingredients. Bring to full boil. Pour into ungreased 2 ½ qt. casserole. Immediately stir in remaining ingredients. Cover tightly. Bake at 375★ for 35 min. remove from oven and let stand for 15 min.

MAIN DISH

Migas Casserole

Al Miller

2 C. of tortilla chips

8 to 12 oz. of Mexican chorizo (or another type of sausage)

2 c. tomato -corn salsa

1c. of onions, chopped.

1 to 2 jalapenos chopped.

2 c. of Monterey jack cheese shredded.

2 eggs

½ c. milk

Salt

Pepper

Pre- heat oven to 350 spray a 9 x 13 glass baking dish with cooking spray

Spread the tortillas chips to the pan in an even layer break down any large pieces of chips.

In a large skillet over medium high heat, cook the chorizo until the oily residue but let it cook for at least 7 min. or so. Add the cooked chorizo to the prepared dish, making sure not to add the oily residue.

In a large bowl, whisk together the eggs, milk garlic powder and salt and pepper. add the egg mixture into the prepared dish.

Top with the cheese and add chopped green onions cover with foil coated with cooking spray bake for 45 to 50 min. let cool for 10 to 15 min. before serving.

Chicken Spaghetti

Genie Thompson

4 Chicken breasts cooked and cut up.
¼ c. Shortening
1 med. Onion
1 tsp. Garlic
½ mushrooms
1 c. tomatoes
Salt
Pepper
Tabasco

Sauté onion in shortening add garlic, mushrooms, tomatoes, chicken, mushroom juice and chicken broth. Simmer 30 mi. Serve over spaghetti

Pizza Casserole

Linda Crownover

1 onion
1 pkg. sliced pepperoni (4 oz.)
⅓ c. butter melted.
6oz. (10-12) thin spaghetti cooked for 10 min. drained.
1 c. (4 oz.) grated swiss cheese 1 lb. mozzarella cheese sliced.
2 cans (8 oz,) tomatoes sauce or less
½ tsp. basil
1 can (4 oz.) mushrooms, drained

Boil pepperoni to remove fat 5 min. drain well. Sauté onion in ½ c. butter until golden brown. Pre-heat oven to 350. pour butter in to 11 x 7 x 2 in. baking dish toss cooked spaghetti in butter and onions over spaghetti with one can of tomatoes sauce. add in order ½ swiss cheese,½ pepperoni ½ mozzarella cheese, all mushrooms sprinkle with oregano and basil add more tomato sauce top with remaining swiss, pepperoni, and mozzarella. Bake in 350 oven 20 to 25 min.

Corn and Chilies

Reva Hensley

1 c. Beswick
1 egg beaten.
2 Tbsp. Sugar
2 Tbsp. melted butter.
½ c. milk
4 oz. can Ortega chilies
½ lb. jack cheese

Mix above ingredients, pour half into casserole dish, mix Ortega chilies, ½ jack cheese over peppers, add another half bake 25 min. at 400.

Meat Loaf

Linda Crownover

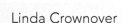

2 lbs. lean ground beef
1 c. old fashioned oats
2 eggs
½ c. ketchup
1 sm. onion chopped.
1 tsp. salt
½ tsp. pepper
¼ c. ketchup

Mix all ingredients except ¼ c. ketchup in a lg. bowl. Press into a 9 x 5 x 3 loaf pan.

Spread remaining ¼ c. ketchup over top bake at 350 for 1 hr. and 15 min. allow to sit a few min. before slicing.

Tamale Pie

Reva Hensley

⅜ c. corn meal
1 tsp. salt
½ c. cold water
1 c. boiling water
¼ lb. pork sausage
½ c. chopped onions.
½ lb. ground beef
1 tsp season salt
2 tsp. chili powder
1 pkg. spaghetti sauce mix
1 ¾ c. tomatoes
2 ½ cans water
1 can whole kernel corn
½ c. pitted olives
½ c. grated cheese

Combine cornmeal, salt, water. add slowly boiling water cook slowly to mush, keep warm, fry sausage and ground beef add onions, ground beef, salt, chili powder, and sauce, blend well, cook 10 min. or till crumbly.

Blend into tomatoes and corn, simmer 20 min. spread meat mixtures in baking 9 x 13 pan. Rubbed garlic spread press olives into top. spread corn meal mush on to add cheese cook at 350 for 45 min.

Lasagna
Martha Pannell

3 lbs. or more ground meat
2 Tbsp. bacon drippings
2 c. onions chopped.
1 or 2 garlic cloves chopped.
2 c. Ro-tell tomatoes.
1 lg. can tomato paste.
2 ½ tsp. salt to taste
1 tsp. Pepper
3 tsp. Oregano
1 lg. carton small curd cottage cheese
1 lb. or more grated mozzarella cheese
1 c. or more grated parmesan cheese

Brown meat in bacon drippings and drain. Add onions, tomatoes and seasonings simmer 30 min. cook 11 or 12 lasagna noodles according to directions. In greased 2 qt. baking disk layer lasagna noodles, sauce and cheese until all used.

Make 2 lg. 2 qt. casseroles. Bake 350 for 30 min. bake 1 hr. and freeze the other for later.

Chicken and Rice Casserole

Linda Crownover

1 can cream of cream of chicken soup.
1 tsp. paprika
1 tsp. onion powder
½ tsp. garlic powder
¼ tsp. oregano
1 c. water
Salt
1 stick butter
1 c. uncooked rice

In a 13 x 9 in pan slice 1 stick of butter over this pour 1 c. dry uncooked rice sprinkle salt. Mix other ingredients, over rice cut up fryer chicken or other meat. Pour the mixture over meat cover with foil and bake in a 325 oven for 2 hrs.

The Recipe for The Beast of Life   Pastor Smith

Begin by adding one" New Heart".

Blend in "God's Word".

Stir frequently with "prayer".

Pour a full cup of the "Holy Ghost" 2 c. if you like a smoother texture.

Add a lg. measure of "God's Love".

And a handful of "grace"

Allow to rise gently, serve yourself, your family, and your world a slice of the best of life! I have tried it, and its joy is unspeakable and full of glory.

Table Grace

We thank you God for happy hearts,
For rain and sunny weather.
We thank you God for this, our food, and that we are together.

Grace

Bless our friends, bless our food, come, O Lord, and sit with us.
May our speech, glow with peace, and your love surround us.
Bless our friends, bless our food, come, O Lord, and be with us.

Chicken Divan

Reva Hensley Via Bonnie Rance

4 chicken breasts cook and pull apart.
2 pkg. frozen broccoli cooked.
1 can cream of mushroom soup.
1 can cream of chicken.
1 c. mayo
½ tsp curry powder
½ c. sharp cheese
½ c. breadcrumbs

Layer chicken breasts and layer of broccoli in 9 x 13 pan. Then mix soups and mayo and curry, pour over chicken and broccoli.

On top of that shred cheese and breadcrumbs. bake 25 to 30 min.in a 350 oven.

Taco Casserole

Linda Spark

3 lbs. hamburger cooked.
1 med. Onion chopped.
1 can cream of mushroom soup.
1 can cream of chicken soup.
7 ½ oz. taco sauce
1 can green chilies
½ lb. shredded cheddar cheese
1 lg. bag of Doritos

Bake in 350 oven for 45 min.

Fry hamburger and onions layer all ingredients in a 9 x 12 baking pan, sprinkle some cheese on top and bake.

Simple Baked Salmon Loaf

Ione Brown

1 ½ C. Milk
1 slice Bread
4 Tbsp. butter
2 cans salmon
2 eggs
½ tsp. salt

Heat milk, bread, and butter in double boiler until creamy. remove bones form salmon beat eggs and mix the salmon with it add milk mixture with it. put in a well-greased loaf pan bake in 350 oven for 1 hr. serve hot or cool.

Fork Tacos
Margaret Ralls Via Bobby Collins

2 lbs. ground beef
8 oz.jar of picante sauce
Lettuce chopped.
Onions chopped.
Tomatoes chopped.

Cook ground beef cooked and drained, add to ground beef 8 oz. jar picante sauce or your favorite sauce. make a bed of lettuce, onions, tomatoes, meet, chips, and cheese and serve.

Hot Crab Cake Sandwiches

Reva Hensley

¾ lb. crab or 1- 6 ½ oz. crab pkg.
Dash of garlic
Dash of celery
2 Tbsp. ground pepper
½ c. mayo
2 tsp. prepared mustard
1 ½ tsp. salt
½ paprika
16 slices sandwich bread
1 pkg pimiento cheese or 8 slices
4 eggs
2 c. milk
1 Tbsp. Worcestershire sauce

Remove crust of bread, mix first 6 ingredients lightly arrange 8 slices of bread in a greased pan. spread mixture over bread. Top each slice of bread to make a sandwich. Beat together eggs, milk, and Worcestershire sauce with salt pour over finished sandwiches moistening entire surface, sprinkle paprika over top.

Refrigerate overnight and bake at 325 for 45 to 60 min.

Ham and Onion Rolls

Reva Hensley

Bisquick
2 c. ground ham
1 c. onion finely chopped.
1 egg
Parsley
Mustard
1 c. white sauce
cheese

make a recipe of Bisquick Biscuits Mix roll out in a rectangle (not as thin as pie crust)

mix 2 c. ground ham, onion chopped egg, parsley, mustard to taste, mix well spread on biscuits dough like jelly roll.

Raises when cooking slice as thick as desired. bake as for biscuits. mix white sauce and cheese heat and pour over rolls.

Easy Pork Chop Casserole

Ione Brown

4 or 5 pork chops ½ "thick
Salt
Pepper
2 Tbsp. fat
1 can cream of mushroom soup.

Brown and season pork chops on both sides in fat in skillet med. Heat. Place browned pork chops in 2 qt. casserole pan. Pour the can cream of mushroom soup over the pork chops, put cover on casserole and bake approximately 40 min. in preheated 375 oven thickly sliced potatoes may also be added for more complete dish.

Meat Balls

1 ½ lb. ground beef
½ or ¾ c. uncooked rice
Onion flakes

Shape into balls place in 9 x 13 in. baking dish cover with 1 or2 cans tomato soup. Bake at 350.

Sweet Meat Balls

Margaret Ralls

3 lbs. hamburger
1lg can evaporated milk.
2 c. quick oats
2 eggs
2 tsp. Salt
½ tsp. Pepper
2 tsp. garlic powder
2 tsp. chili powder
2 c. ketchup
2 tsp. liquid smoke
1 ½ c. sugar
½ tsp. garlic salt

Mix well put in pan after rolled into balls. Bake at 350 oven till done
pour sauce over meat balls. Bake 1 hr. at 350.

Lemon Rosemary Chicken

Loria Flynn via Charles Norton

1pkg. chicken breast
Rosemary
½ lemon juice
½ lb. butter
Season salt
1 bottle Corona beer

Take chicken put in baking pan, pour corona over it, pour lemon juice over it, ground up rosemary and sprinkle over chicken and season salt cut butter up and put on the chicken. bake in 350 oven for 45 to 60 min. till chickens done.

Tuna Casserole

Mrs. Betty Hodge

2 C. tuna packed in water.
1 lg. can chaw main noodles.
1 can cream of mushroom soup.
½ c. pimento
½ lb. broken cashews
¾ c. milk
½ onion chopped.
½ celery chopped.

Mix all together using ½ of noodles place in greased baking dish top with remaining noodles bake at 350 for 40 min.

Mexican Chicken

Vernice Boyed

1 lg. fryer – cut up.
1 can cream of mushroom soup.
1 can cream of chicken soup.
1 can Ro-tel tomatoes and green chilies
1 can chicken broth.

Combine soup and tomatoes, then add 1 med. Chopped onion. Simmer 5 min. add 1 tsp. oregano and 1 tsp. chili powder, set aside. In a 3 qt casserole pan alternate layers of chicken with cheese flavored Doritos lg bag. Add 1 lb. sharp cheese shredded pour sauce over this and bake at 350 about 45 min. or until chicken is tender. (you can make this and freeze it)

Barbeque

Linda Crownover

Beef roast
Pork roast
1 lg. can (15 oz.) tomato sauce
½ c. barbeque season
4 Tbsp. brown sugar
4 Tbsp. lemon juice
2 Tbsp. liquid smoke
2 Tbsp. Worcestershire

Cook all day 300 oven (covered pan) place roast in averaged roast. mix all ingredients together, pour over meat, cook 6 to 8 hrs. in over (covered Pan). When done stir with fork–remove bones.

Pizza Spaghetti Casserole

Margaret Ralls

⅓ c. butter
1 onion chopped.
1- 4oz. pkg. pepperoni
10 oz. cooked spaghetti
4 oz. mozzarella
8 oz. tomato sauce
½ tsp. oregano
4 oz. can drain mushroom.

Preheat oven to 350.

Boil pepperoni for 5 min. place on paper towel to drain.

Cook onions in butter stir into the spaghetti pour into lg. baking dish top with ½ oz. of the pepperoni and ½ of the cheese add all the mushrooms oregano and basil and tomato sauce add the remaining pepperoni, swiss cheese and top with mozzarella cheese bake for 20 – 25 min.

Country Pie Casserole   R. Quetone

½ 8 oz. can (½) tomato sauce
½ c. breadcrumbs
1 lb. ground beef
¼ chopped pepper.
1 ½ tsp. salt
⅛ tsp. oregano
4 tsp. pepper

Filling_____
1 ⅓ c. minute rice
1 c. water
1 ½ 8oz. c. (1 ½ c.) tomato sauce
1 c. grated cheese(cheddar)
½ tsp. salt

Combine these ingredients and mix well, Pat meat mixture into the bottom of pie plate and pinch 1" fluting around edges of greased 9" pie plate.

filling_____
combine all the above ingredients save ¼ c. cheese. Spoon rice mixture into meat shell, cover with foil. bake at 350 for 25 min. uncover and sprinkle top with remaining cheese return to oven uncovered and bake 10 -15 min. cut into pie shaped prices.

The Forgotten Roast

Pat Hauser

Roasts
Lipton dry onion soup mix
2 can water
1 can cream of mushroom soup.

Place in roaster, cover with one pkg. Lipton dry onion soup mix, add 1 can cream of mushroom soup,2 cans water. cover the roast with 2 layers of foil place the lid over this. Cook 4 hrs. at 350 add no salt as onion soup is salty enough. Makes its own gravy and you do not need to worry about it for 4 hrs.

Sauce for Open Faced Hamburger   Genie Thompson

1 lg. onion chopped.
3 Tbsp. oil
3 Tbsp. flour
2 c. liquid
Chicken broth
Tomato juice
Dash lea & Perrins
Dash Maggi season
Salt
Pepper
Dash Tabasco

Sauce for open faced hamburger, sauté onions until brown in 3 Tbsp. oil dust onion with 3 Tbsp. flour and brown. Add 2 c. liquid, chicken broth and tomato juice, dash lea & Perrins's sauce, dash of seasoning to taste stir until thickened add more water if needed.

Chicken Rice Casserole

Jennie Best

1 Tbsp. chopped onion.

1 – 14oz can chicken broth

1 – 5 oz. can chicken

1 c. shredded cheese

½ c. uncooked rice

1 ½ qt. casserole pan, cover and bake at 375 oven for one hr.

Super Nachos

Reva Hensley

1 lb. ground beef
½ lb. chorizo sausage
1 lg. onions chopped.
Salt
Liq. Hot pepper
1 or 2 cans refried beans.
1 – 4 oz. can whole green chilies chunks chopped
Sprinkle chilies
2 or 3 c. shredded jack or mild cheddar
¾ c. taco sauce
Green onions
1 c. pitted ripe olives.
1 avocado mashed
1 c. sour cream
8 c. fried tortilla pieces

Cook and brown sausage and beef, add lg. onion chopped cook on heat stirring till lightly browned season with salt and if desired add liquid hot pepper seasoning to suit your taste, spread 1 or 2 cans 1 lb. each refried beans in casserole dish top meat chop 1 can 4oz. whole green chicks sprinkle over beans and meat mixture. Cover evenly with 2 or 3 c. shredded cheese jack or mild cheddar cheese or both measure ¾ c. prepared taco sauce, drizzle over the cheese cover and chill if made ahead bake uncovered in a 400 oven for 20 – 25 min. or until hot.

Garnish with chopped green onions and 1 c. pitted ripe olives. In the center 1 avocado mashed with sour cream. Tuck 8 cups fried tortilla pieces around edges to make petaled flavor effects scoop up be mixture with tortilla pieces.

Oven Porcupine Meat Balls

Beverly King

1 lb. ground beef
½ c. uncooked regular rice
½ c. water
½ c. chopped onion.
1 tsp. salt
½ tsp. celery salt
1 tsp. garlic powder
⅛ tsp. pepper
1 can 15 oz. tomato sauce
1 c. water
2 tsp. Worcestershire sauce

Heat oven to 350 mix. Meat, rice, ½ c. water, the onion, salt, garlic powder, and pepper shape mixture by rounded tablespoon full into balls place meat balls into ungreased baking dish (8 x 8 x 2) stir together reaming ingredients pour over meat balls cover with foil bake 45 min. uncover bake 15 mi. Longer.

Easy Deep-Dish Pizza

Vernice Boyd

3 c. Bisques baking mix.
¾ c. water
1 lb. ground beef
1 c. onion chopped.
½ tsp. salt
2 cloves garlic crushed.
1 can (15 oz.) tomato sauce
1 tsp. Italian seasoning
1 jar (4 ½ oz.) sliced mushrooms, drained.
½ c. chopped green peppers.
2 c. shredded mozzarella cheese

Heat oven to 425 lightly greased jelly roll pan 15 ½ x 10 ½ inch or cookie sheet. Mix baking mix and water until soft dough forms, pat dough on bottom and sides of pan. With floured hands.

Cook and stir ground beef, onions, salt, and garlic until beef is browned drain. Mix tomato sauce and Italian seasoning, spread evenly over dough. Spoon beef mixture over sauce. Top with mushrooms, green pepper and cheese. Bake until crust is golden brown about 20 min.

Chicken Broccoli Shells and Cheese   Loria Flynn

8 oz. pasta shells (3 c. dried shells)
2 Tbsp. canola oil
1 lb. boneless, skinless chicken breasts, diced.
1 (16oz.) bag frozen broccoli florets
¼ c. all – purpose flour
1 c. 2% low-fat milk
1c.chricken broth
1 tsp. garlic powder
1 tsp. black pepper
2 c. shredded cheddar cheese

Prepare pasta according to package direction drain and set aside.

In lg, deep pot, heat oil over med. high. Add chicken and cook 5 – 7 mins. Add broccoli and cook 5 -7 mins. Until chickens cooked throughout and broccoli is warm remove chicken and broccoli from skillet.to stove, reducing heat to med. add flour and stir continuously for 1 min. slowly add milk, broth, garlic powder, and pepper to skillet. Cook until sauce is thick and bubbly, stirring occasionally. Stir in cheese until melted. Add pasta, chicken and broccoli to pot. stir to combine. MAKE SURE CHICKEN IS WELL DONE. BEFORE ADDING TO POT.!!!!

Shepherd's Pie

Loria Flynn

2 lg. potatoes with skin, chopped.
⅓ c. milk
½ lb. ground meat
2 Tbsp. flour
1 pkg. frozen mixed vegetable
1 can veg, stock.

Place diced potato in saucepan. Cover with water and bring to a boil. Reduce heat and simmer(about 15 mins.) drain potatoes and mash. Stir in milk and set aside.

Pre – heat oven to 375. Brown meat in a lg. skillet. Stir in flour and cook for 1 min., stirring constantly.

Add vegetables and broth. Bring to slow boil. spoon vegetables /meat mixture into8 inch square baking dish. Spread potatoes over mixture bake 25 mins.

Serve hot. Garnish with shredded cheese.

Chicken Pot Pie with Vegies   Loria Flynn

2 pie crust
2 cans cream of potato soup 2 cans cream of celery soup
2 cans (15oz.) veg. all drain.
4 c. chicken cooked and chopped.
½ c. milk
2 tsp. thyme
½ tsp. pepper

Take rotisserie chicken or 6 to 7 chicken breast)

Use a 9 x 13 in. casserole pan set out the tub frozen crusts to throw. Cook and chopped chicken mix all ingredients together in lq. Bowl. Season to taste pour into dish. Top with 2 crusts, pinching seam down middle and using fork to cramp the edge. Cutting any extra and making a few slits in top of pie. bake at 350 till bubbly and browned cover with tin foil if it is getting too brown or to bubbly. Let cool and serve after to mins.

Chicken Kiev

Loria Flynn

1 Tbsp. butter
1 tsp. parsley
6 to 8 boneless chicken breasts
Breadcrumbs
Egg wash(2 eggs,½ c. milk, mix well)
2 cloves fresh garlic

½ c. butter, softened. flatten chicken breasts, using a meat mallet. Being a careful not to tear the meat mix the first four ingredients well and place a generous amount in the center of breast. Roll up chicken breast ensuring that the butter mixture is enclosed with in the breast. You may need to wash then coat with breadcrumbs, covering all the meat place breast in freezer about ½ hr. to dry breadcrumbs before baking.

Heat 3 in. of cooking oil in pan. Do not overheat, otherwise the outside will burn, and the inside want cook. usually takes 9 – 14 min. depending on the size of the breast. Place chicken breast on a bed of wild rice with buttered carrots and onions.

Irish Corned Beef
Loria Flynn

3 lbs. corned beef
6 pepper corns
2sm, onion, quartered.
2 bay leaves
1 med. head of cabbage
8 sm. new potatoes

Place corned beef in heavy saucepan with pepper corns, onions and bay leaves. Cover meat with water and bring rapidly to boil. Low heat. remove any fat. cover pan and simmer until meat is tender, about 2 hrs. quarter cabbage and add potatoes add to meat. Cook and additional 15 to 20 mins. Add any other vegetables you like, and cook tell meat and vegetables are finished cooking tell the vegetables are tender to your liking as well as the meat.

Stuff Peppers

Loria Flynn

6 sm. green bell peppers, cleaned.
1 lb. ground beef
2 Eggs
Rice
1 sm. onion finely chopped.
Ketchup
Garlic
Salt
Pepper
Worcestershire sauce

Mix all ingredients put into clean bell peppers bake at 375. Tell meat is completely cooked and peppers are tender. Top with ketchup and cook tell baked in. serve warm.

Mexican Meatloaf

Loria Flynn

2 lbs. ground beef
1 c. corn chips, coarsely crushed.
⅓ c. taco sauce
1 egg, beaten.
Dash tabasco sauce
2 Tbsp. taco seasoning
½ c, grated cheddar cheese
½ c. grated Monterey jack cheese

Combine all ingredients and shape into a loaf pan. Put in oven at 375. Until all is cooked till meat is done to your liking.

Chillipa Dinner Bowls

Loria Flynn

1 lb. pinto beans – dry
1 (3 ½ lbs.) bone in pork loin roast
1 Tbsp. chili powder
2 can green chilies(chopped)
2 cloves garlic (minced)
Salt
1 tsp. oregano
1 tsp. cumin
32 oz. chicken broth
1 bottle V-8 juice
1 can diced tomatoes and green chilies (whatever temp. you want)

Soak beans over night and cook all the next day. tell tender and thickened.

Pre-heat oven 350 for about 5 hrs. after about 2 hrs. remove the bone and shred the meat by pulling apart with 2 forks… make taco shell bowls and serve this in them. Serve with vegetables and sauce on top with sour cream or any other toppings you like.

Burritos

Loria Flynn

1 lb. ground beef, browned.
2 (12oz) cans refried beans
1 pk. Cheddar cheese, shredded.
1 pkg. taco seasoning
Flour tortillas

Mix ground beef and taco seasoning together cook down mix in refried beans, warm tortillas on the stove or in microwave add cheese on top of meat mixture, add vegetables on that if wanted. Put on cookie sheet put in oven to melt cheese then serve.

Chicken Enchiladas
Loria Flynn and Johnny Flynn

4 med boneless skinless chicken breast
1 (4 oz.) can green chilies chopped.
2 (10 ¾) oz. cans cream of mushrooms soup
Corn tortillas
1 c. shredded cheddar cheese
Sour cream
Olives
Salsa

In slow cooker combine chicken, cream of mushroom soup, chilies, cover cook on low for 4 ½ hrs. stirring each hr. remove chicken and cut into bite sized pieces. Place chicken on top tortillas, making sure equal amount in each. With chilies and cheese and roll up place in pan in oven till cheese melted bake at 350 for 15 to 20 mins. Garnish with cheese or whatever you want.

Pork Chop Casserole

Frieda Kowalski

4 debone pork chops.
6 med Potatoes sliced.
1 med. onion slices
2 cans cream of mushroom soup

Put browned pork chops in a 2 qt. baking dish mix in potatoes onions and soup.

Cook till all vegetables too desired tenderness.

Orgasmic chicken
Johnny Flynn

4 lg. chicken breast
3 garlic cloves
½ to ¾ c. butter
3 Tbsp. lemon juice

Cook slowly in oven at 375. Cover chicken breast with butter and garlic and lemon juice. Tell tender and juice and done.

New England Broil
Loria Flynn

Small roast or lg. stack
6 med. Potatoes
1 med. Onion
4 Carrots
2 Garlic cloves
½ gal. Water

Put roast in roaster combine all in oven at 350. For 2 hrs. cover or tell desired tenderness and meat to desired doneness.

Beef Jambalaya

Loria Flynn

2 c. sausage, diced.
2 med. onions coarsely chopped.
2 stalks celery, sliced.
½ green bell pepper, seeded and diced.
½ red bell pepper, seeded and diced.
1 (28 oz.) can diced tomatoes
3 cloves garlic diced.
1 Tbsp. parsley diced.
½ tsp. thyme leaves
2 whole cloves
1 c. raw long grained converted rice
1 lbs. beef browned.

In slow cooker, thoroughly mix all ingredients cover and cook on low for 8 to 10 hrs. then serve with corn bread or garlic bread.

Beef Enchiladas

Loria Flynn

1 lb. ground beef, browned.
½ c. onion, chopped.
1 c. enchilada sauce
1 Tbsp. oil
8 to 10 corn tortillas
10 oz. cheddar cheese, shredded.
8 oz. Monterey jack cheese shredded.
8 oz. sour cream

Cook ground beef until browned and onion is tender. Add enchilada sauce to meat simmer for 30 min. cover the bottom of a skillet with oil when the oil is hot, cook tortillas lightly on both sides. As soon as removed from heat, spoon meat mixture, sour cream, add cheese onto tortillas. Roll up tortillas and place side by side in a 9 x 13 cake pan cover the tortillas with remaining cheese and sauce. Bake at 35 for 1 hr.

BBQ Spareribs

Loria Flynn

3 to 4 lbs. spareribs
3 sm. onions finely sliced.
2 Tbsp. vinegar
2 Tbsp. Worcestershire sauce
1 Tbsp. salt
1 tsp. paprika
½ tsp. red pepper
1 tsp. chili powder
¾ c. ketchup
¾ c. water
½ tsp. honey

Cut meaty spareribs into servings. Sprinkle with salt and pepper. Place in a roster pan and cover with onions. Combine remaining ingredients and pour over meat and bake at 350 for 1 ½ hrs. baste occasionally, turning spareribs once or twice. Remove cover from roaster during last 15 mins. Of baking to brown spareribs.

Gumbo

Loria Flynn

½ lb. smoked sausage sliced.

1 c. onion finely sliced.

½ c. green pepper finely sliced.

¾ c. all – purpose flour

½ c. celery, finely chopped.

8 c. water

2 garlic cloves, minced.

1 bay leaf

1 ½ tsp. Cajun seasoning

1 tsp. salt

½ tsp. salt

½ tsp. dried thyme

¼ tsp. pepper

Tabasco sauce dash

4 c. rice cooked.

¾ c. green onion

Brown sausage and vegetables, combine meat mixture with flour and water with seasonings cook 6 to 8 hrs. on high add rice cook for 3 to 4 hrs. tell rice is soft. serve with garlic bread or corn bread.

Loria's Fajitas

Loria Flynn

1 ½ lb. beef or chicken
1 sm. onion finely sliced.
½ tsp. pepper
1 bell pepper cleaned and finely sliced.
1 clove garlic, minced.
1 tsp. season salt
1 tsp. chili pepper
1 tsp. salt
Meat tenderizer

Sliced meat in strips and vegetables cook meat till thoroughly cooked add sliced vegetables brown till tender. Mix with seasonings serve with tortilla and beans and rice.

BBQ Pork

Loria Flynn

2 onions, sliced.
4 to 5 lbs. pork roast
5 to 6 cloves
2 c. water
1(18oz.) bottle BBQ sauce

Put half of sliced onions in bottom of a slow cooker, add meat cloves and water, Top with remaining onion. Cover and cook overnight on low for 8 to 12 hrs. remove bone and fat from meat. Put meat back into the slow cooker add chopped onion and BBQ sauce cover and cook on low for 8-12 hrs. or on high for 3 – 5 hrs. stirring 2 to 3 times.

Southern Fried Catfish

8 (5 or 6 oz.) catfish fillets
Salt
Crab boil seasoning
4 c. all – purpose flour
1 c. cornmeal
Oil

Heat a frying pan or fryer fill with oil to 350. take skin off both sides of fish, mix corn meal and flour with seasonings mix well roll fish in it and place in fryer or skillet. Cook tell crisp and fish is flakey when picked with a fork. Or floats on top of oil in fryer. Drain 7 to 8 mins on paper towel.

BREAD & ROLLS

.

Hot Rolls

Nelly Tuck

1 cake yeast
1 C. warm water
2 c. scalded milk
2 tsp. shortening
2 tsp. sugar
1 tsp. salt

Soak 1 c.in 1c. warm water, scold 2 milk when cooled add to yeast and water. 2 tsp. shortening, 2 tsp. sugar, tsp. salt, beat flour in until stiff enough for biscuit dough cover let rise until twice it sizes then stir down and make into rolls, about 1 or 1 ½ hrs. before ready to bake and set for rising after rise cook in 400 oven for 20 min. or until golden brown.

Bread Pudding

Fern Whitby

2 beaten eggs.
¾ c. sugar
1 tsp. vanilla
½ tsp. nutmeg
½ tsp. cinnamon
1 can carnation cream
1 lg. vanilla instant pudding
2 c. milk
¾ c. butter
12 slices of bread

Break bread in baking dish in a lg. bowl mix, 2 eggs, sugar, vanilla, nutmeg, nutmeg, cinnamon, make lg. instant pudding, the finish with milk. Pour in pan over bread, melt butter over mixture sprinkle with sugar. Bake at 350 until done.

Mexican Cornbread

Margaret Ralls

2 pkg. dry yeast
1 Tbsp. salt
1 Tbsp. sugar
½ tsp. soda
1 c. butter milk
1 c. corn meal
½ tsp. butter
½ c. oil
1 med. onion chopped.
1 c. cream style corn
2 chilies chopped.
1 ½ sharp cheddar cheese grated.
5 c. all-purpose flour

Mix yeast, soda corn meal in lg. mixing bowl, heat oil, salt, sugar, onion, and butter milk until warm, stir into meal mixture add eggs and beat well add corn, pepper, and cheese. Add flour 1 c. at a time turn dough out and knead until smooth grease dough and bowl with a little butter, cover and let rise in warm place until, double in size (about 1 ½ hrs. Punch down dough and knead lightly 2- or 3-min. shape into loaf pans allow to rise double in size again bake at 350 till golden brown about 25 – 30 mi. Remove from pan brush with melted butter when cool wrap in foil and store. freeze well and makes excellent ham and cheese sandwiches.

Dumplings

Ione Brown

2 c. self – rising flour
⅓ to ½ c. milk
3 Tbsp. Melted shortening
1 egg

Beat egg until smooth add milk and melted shortening, mix thoroughly, pour liquid into the self- rising flour and mix to an incredibly soft dough.

Drop by spoon fouls onto boiling broth or slightly thickened stew cover tightly and cook 10 to 14 min.

Beer Bread

Al Miller

3 c. self – raising flour.
2 Tbsp. sugar
1 – 12 oz. can of warm beer

Mix and pour into greased loaf pans. Bake at 350 for 40 min. pour ½ cube melted butter over top return to oven and bake 20 min. maybe longer. Till golden brown.

Noodle Casserole

Reva Hensley

1 (12oz.) pkg. noodles
1 (16 oz.) carton cottage cheese
1 sour cream
1 c. thinly sliced onion
2 tsp. salt
1 tsp. pepper
1 tsp. cayenne pepper
1 tsp. monosodium
⅛ tsp. cayenne pepper

12 oz. pkg. noodles, cook and drain, 16oz carton cottage cheese 1 c. sour cream, 1 c. thickly sliced green onion, ½ c. milk, 2 tsp. salt, ¼ tsp. pepper, 1 tsp. cayenne pepper 1 tsp. monosodium glutamate, ⅛ tsp. cayenne pepper.

Mix well all ingredients together carefully pour into 2 qt. casserole dish bake, covered in pre heated 350 for 1 hr. or till heated all way through and bubbly.

Popovers

Martha Pannell

2 eggs
1 c. milk
1 c. sifted flour
1 tsp. salt

Mix with spoon just well blended disregard lumps.

Fill well-greased 5oz. glass custard cups ¾ full, set in pan for easy handling. Place in cold oven set 450 turn on heat. do not open oven for 30 min. popovers should be tall and brown.

Yeast Rolls

Ione Brown

½ c. sweet milk
1 egg, beaten.
1 pkg. yeast
1 ½ Tbsp. sugar
2 Tbsp. shortening
2 ½ c. sifted self – rising flour

Add beaten egg to milk and mix with yeast and sugar, dissolve in the warm water.

Cut shortening into the flour mix the liquids and flour to form a soft ball dough.

Kneed gently on well-floured board. roll about ⅜ in. thick cut with a lg. biscuits cutter. Brush the tops with melted butter. And fold to form pocketbook rolls. Place on greased baking tin cover with towel allow to rise for 1 to 2 hrs. at room temp. until double in size bake at 400 for 10 to 15 min.

To give the rolls a pleasing brown crust brush the tops with melted butter or sweet milk. Makes 12 – 14 rolls.

If you pinch rolls off the big dough ball can make more rolls.

Batter Rolls

Juanita Carlile

1 ¼ c. milk (scold)
2 ½ Tbsp. sugar
1 ½ tsp. salt
¼ c. luck warm water
2 pkgs. Yeast
¼ c. shortening.
1tsp. sugar
3 ½ c. flour all-purpose sifted

Mix scolded milk, sugar, salt and shortening cool to luck warm. Mix in luck warm water, sugar 2 pkgs. yeast.

Let stand until dissolved stir add luck warm mixture of milk add flour stir only enough to dampen flour fill well-greased muffin pans half full cover with clean towel let rise in warm place. Free from draft until double in size about 35 min.

Bake in oven at 425 about 20 min. remove while still warm remove from pans.

Easy Refrigerator Rolls

Reba Quetone

2 c. boiling water
1 c. sugar
1 tsp. salt
2 eggs beaten.
2 yeasts (dried cakes)
1 c. luck warm water
4 c. flour

Mix boiling water, salt, shortening cool to luck warm. Soften yeast cakes in luck warm water. Add sugar when dissolved stir into 1ˢᵗ mixture add beaten eggs stir in flour mix well until smooth do not kneed cover and place in frig. Until ready to use make out rolls and let rise 3 hrs. bake at 400 till golden brown. About 15 min.

Banana Nut Bread

Nancy P. Burnett

½ c. shortening.
1 c. sugar
2 eggs
1 tsp. buttermilk
2 mashed bananas
Pinch of salt
2 c. flour
½ c. nuts

Set oven at 350, cream ½ c. shortening,1 c. sugar. Add 2 eggs, 1 tsp. buttermilk,2 bananas pinch of salt. Mix thoroughly add 2 c. flour, ½ c. nuts. Bake 1 hr. in greased loaf pan.

Chocolate Rolls

Margaret Ralls

5 eggs separated.
1 c. sugar
3 Tbsp. cocoa
2 Tbsp. flour
1 tsp. vanilla
Pinch salt
2-pint whipping cream

Beat yolks till creamy, add sugar, then cocoa and flour, add vanilla and salt, fold in egg whites which have been beaten to stiff picks, pour this on cookie sheet lined with wax paper which has been greased on both sides. Bake 20 min. at 350 turn out on damp towel cover with whipped cream then roll up like a jelly roll store in refrigerator slice when firm.

Pepperoni Rolls

Loria Flynn

Bag of yeast rolls or crescent rolls
Pepperoni slices
Mozzarella cheese
Pizza sauce or spaghetti sauce

Take rolls spread out put pepperoni and cheese on center and roll up with cheese in center. Continue till are gone, let rise till double in size. put in oven after and cook 20 min or till golden brown.

Cherry Dumplings

Ione Brown

1 ½ c. flour
1 ½ Tbsp. butter
1 ½ tsp. baking powder
1 ¼ tsp. salt
½ c. milk
Cherries
2 c. sugar
Butter

Make a biscuit dough using, roll and cut dough in large circle's fill each with drained cherries (2 Tbsp. in each dumpling) bring up the sides over the cherries and pinch the dough together. Place in deep baking dish, cover with 2 c. sugar and butter cover with boiling water overall. until the dish is half full bake 1 hr. at 375.

Ham Rolls
Jeannie Best

4oz. pkg. long boiled ham
1 sm. Jar chopped ripe olives.
8 oz. pkg. cream cheese
2 Tbsp. chopped onions.

Mix last three ingredients and spread on slices of boiled ham. Roll into pin wheels. wrap in wax paper slice when thoroughly chilled.

Apple Dumplings
Loria Flynn

1 can crescent rolls
1 lg. granny smith apples
¾ c. sugar
Sm. Can mountain dew soda
1 stick butter
Cinnamon
Sugar to sprinkle

Heat oven to 350, slice and core into 8 slices unroll crescent roll dough. Place one slice apple in each roll fold sides up on apple to completely cover. Start at bogger4 part of roll and roll completely. Put in baking pan 9 x 13 in. cook butter and sugar until thick pour over the apple crescent roll sprinkle with cinnamon and sugar to taste. pour mountain dew in the corn of pan (not over rolls themselves) bake at 350 for about 25 min. or until golden brown.

Apple Dumplings

Ione Brown

Apple
½ C. Sugar
1 ½ tsp. cinnamon
1 Tbsp. butter
6 apple corded.
1 c. sugar
2 cups water
3 Tbsp. water
¼ c. brown sugar
3 Tbsp. butter
¼ c. brown sugar
3 Tbsp. Butter
¼ c. brown sugar

Make crust for double crust pie, roll to about ⅛ in. thick on large flour board. Cut in 6 pieces and put a pat of butter on each place a mixture of apples and cinnamon and apple cavities. Dot with 1 Tbsp butter.

Fold pastry over each apple by bringing corners of dough together. Press and moisten edges lightly, turn upside down in baking pan. Heat 1 c. sugar,2c. water and 3Tbsp. ¼ c. brown sugar to almost boiling. And sprinkle brown sugar and cinnamon over top. Pour this hot syrup over and around dumplings. Bake to 425 for 10 min., the lower heat to 350 and bake about 30 min. until bubbling and brown. Serve with milk or cream.

All Souls Day Bread

Loria Flynn

4 yeast cakes (fertility and money)
2 C. milk
8 c. all – purpose flour (fertility and money)
1 tsp. salt (protection)
8 egg yolks (fertility)
2 c. sugar (love)
1 tsp. grated orange peel (love and Money)
1 grated lemon peel (protection)
½ c. butter
1 tsp. poppy seeds (luck and invisibility)

Dissolve yeast in ½ c. milk, add 1 c. flour sprinkle a little flour on top and let rise until doubled in size. Add salt, egg yolks, beat until thick. Add sugar and peels and mix other ingredients. Add 2 c. flour and remaining milk alternating each so it does not get to dry or to wet. knead for 5 to 10 mins. Add remaining flour and butter, knead until dough comes away from hands. Set dough in a warm dry place, cover with a warm damp cloth, until it rises to double in size. Separate into 4 parts. Roll out and braid, brush top with beaten egg yolks and sprinkle with poppy seeds let rise bake at 350 for 1 hr.

Pumpkin Bread

Loria Flynn

1 ¾ c. all – purpose flour (fertility and money)
1 ½ c. sugar (love and passion)
¾ tsp. salt(protection)
1tsp. baking soda
½ tsp. ground cinnamon (spirituality and protection)
½ tsp. ground nutmeg (luck and health)
1 c. canned pumpkin(abundance)
⅓ c. water(cleansing)
2 lg. eggs(fertility)
1 tsp. vanilla (love and mental prowess)
½ c. veg. oil
½ c. chopped walnuts (health and wishes will counter act fertility spell)
Confectioners' sugar

Combine all dry ingredients in a lg. bowl. Mix well. In different bowl, combine all wet ingredients, mix well. Add dry ingredients slowly and beat thoroughly stir in nuts and pour batter into greased loaf pan. Bake at 350 for 75 to 80 mins. But watch your time as different ovens may lengthen or shorten time. Cool 15 min. before removing from pan. Sprinkle with sugar if desired.

Banana Tea Bread

Margaret Ralls

1 ⅔ c. all – purpose flour

2 eggs, beaten.

1 tsp. soda

½ tsp. salt

1 c. bananas, mashed (3 sm. bananas)

½ c. butter, softened.

½ c. sour cream

1 c. sugar

½ c. chopped nuts (optional)

Pre-heat oven to 350. Combine dry ingredients set aside.

In lg bowl cream together wet ingredients on high speed on mixer for 2 mins. Add dry ingredients slowly and mix to smooth and add bananas, sour cream and nuts beat on low for 30 seconds or until well blended.

Pour batter into greased loaf pans or bunt pans.

Bake 350 for 45 to 55 mins. Until bread test done with toothpick. Cool 10 mins. The remove from pan. Cool thoroughly before slicing.

Blueberry Muffins
Loria Flynn

2 c. all – purpose flour
¼ c. sugar
3 tsp. salt
1 egg, well beaten.
1 c. milk
¼ c. butter, melted.
1 c. or ¾ c. frozen or fresh blueberries

Heat oven to 400, line muffin tins with paper baking cups or spray with pan spray.

In med bowl combine first 4 ingredients stir in remaining ingredients until moistened spoon batter into prepared muffin cups filling to ⅔ full bake for 20 to 25 mins. Or golden brown.

Banana Bread

Loria Flynn

1 c. sugar
1 c. bananas, mashed.
½ c. milk
1 tsp. vanilla
2 eggs
2 c. all – purpose flour
½ c. nuts
1 tsp. soda
½ tsp. salt
¾ tsp. cinnamon
½ tsp. nutmeg

Heat oven to 350 grease loaf pan cook 45 to 60 mins. Until toothpick comes out clean.

Ice Cream Muffins Loria Flynn

2 c. vanilla ice cream, softened.
1 egg
2 Tbsp. oil
2 c. all – purpose flour

Combine the ice cream, egg and oil in a bowl. Mix in the flour. Fill muffin cups ⅔ full bake the muffins at 425 for 20 to 25 mins. Let them cool and put on frosting if you like.

(Cheekos LaCabia Rolls Pastry)   Reva Hensley and Bonnie

Breakfasts Kola or Nut and Poppy Seed Rolls
4 ½ c. all – purpose flour
1 tsp. salt
1 c. warm water
½ c. butter
2 eggs
4 Tbsp. sugar
2 yeast cakes
Poppy seed filling

Crumble yeast into a bowl add warm water and sugar let stand until dissolved.

Mix butter and flour as for a pie crust. Make a hole in the mixture and egg yolks, salt and yeast mix. Mix until smooth and dough leaves side of bowl.

Divide into 4 pieces and roll as thin as possible spread nut filling.

Place on greased pan and brush with egg white after you roll it up let stand in warm place for 1 hr. bake at 350 for 30 to 45 mins. Until brown cover with a damp cloth as soon as out of oven for 10 mins. To make a nice crust.

Herbed Biscuits

Loria Flynn

2 c. all – purpose flour
4 tsp. baking powder
½ tsp salt
1 Tbsp. fresh rosemary
½ c. butter, room temperature
⅔ c. milk
1 egg

Sift dry ingredients into a mixing bowl. Cut in butter as for a pie crust, then add the milk and egg. Mix until you have moistened but not over mixed.

Roll out dough on floured surface roll to about ¼ inch thick. Cut with a glass or cutter place on cookie sheet and bake in a 350 oven for 20 to 30 mins. Or till golden brown.

DESSERTS

Quick Cobbler

Al Miller

¼ c. butter
1 c. sugar
1 c. milk
1 c. flour
1 tsp. baking powder

While butter is melting in cobbler pan in oven mix sugar with milk, flour and baking powder. Pour into pan, add can of fruit which has been sweetened to taste bake at 350 until brown.

Lemon Cheese Pie

Linda Crownover

---1ˢᵗ-------------
2 c. sugar
1 Tbsp. flour
1 Tbsp. cornmeal

----2ⁿᵈ. --------------
4 eggs unbeaten
¼ c. milk
4 Tbsp. grated lemon rind
¼ c. lemon juice

Mix sugar, flour, cornmeal tosses lightly with fork. Mix remaining ingredients and add to above mixture. Beat until smooth, pour into unbaked pie shell (9oz.) bake 35-40 min. at 375.

Apple Cake

Barbara Anderson

2 c. chopped apples.
½ c. shortening.
1 tsp. soda
1 c. sifted flour
1 egg
1 c sugar
1 tsp. cinnamon
½ c. nuts optional

Cream shortening, sugar and eggs, sift soda, cinnamon and flour into above add apples and nuts. if desired.

Bake at 325-degree oven.

Frozen Pineapple Dessert

Carolyn Duncan via Joyce Dye

Enough vanilla wafers crumbled.
Enough melted butter
1 lg. can crush pineapple.
1 c. eagle brand milk
½ tsp. lemon juice

Enough vanilla wafers crumbled for bottom of pan. Add enough melted butter to make crumbs sticks together cover bottom of pan. Mix the 3 above ingredients together and pour over crumbled wafers crumble vanilla wafers over tax freeze and serve.

Hot Fudge Sunday Cake
Barbara Anderson

1 c. flour
¾ c. sugar
2 Tbsp. cocoa
1 tsp. vanilla
1 c. chopped nuts.
1 c. brown sugar
¼ c. cocoa
2 tsp. baking powder
¼ tsp salt
½ c. milk
2 Tbsp. salad oil
1 ¾ c. hottest tap water
Favorite ice cream

Heat oven to 350 ungreased (9 x9x 2 in.) pan stir together flour, cocoa, baking powder and salt. mix in milk, oil and vanilla until smooth. Stir in nuts, spread evenly in pan sprinkle with brown sugar and cocoa ¼ c. each. Pour hot water over batter bake 40 min. let stand 15 min. spoon into dishes top with ice cream spoon sauce over top.

Crushed Pineapple Cake

Barbara Anderson

_cake_____
2 c. flour
2 tsp. soda
½ tsp. salt
1 ½ c. sugar
2 c. crushed pineapple
¼ c. oil
½ c. each
Brown sugar
Nuts
Coconut
__icing_____
¾ c. sugar
½ c. melnot
1 stick butter
Boil for 1 min. pour over hot cake.

Mix all the cake ingredients together put in a greased and lightly flour pan (9 x 13)

bake at 350,45 to 55 min., before icing -make holes on top of hot cake make syrup for top of hot cake and pour over it.

½ c. each brown sugar, nuts and coconut

256

Bisquick Cobbler

2 Tbsp. butter
1 c. Bisquick
½ c. sugar
½ c. milk
3 c. cut up fruit can be fresh, frozen, thawed, or canned.

DO NOT USE CANNED FRUIT PIE FILLING

Melt 2 Tbsp. butter in 8 x8 in. baking pan. Mix Bisquick, sugar and milk pour over melted butter. Spoon fruit over Bisquick mixture. If using canned fruit, you can pour some juice also.

Holy Cow Cake

Chocolate cakes mix bake as directed on box.
1 – 14 oz. can sweeten condensed milk
8 oz. jar of caramel ice cream topping
4 – 5 butter finger candy bars crushed
1 – 8 oz. cream cheese, softened
12 oz. cool whip.

Prepare and bake cake as directed on package meanwhile, blend caramel and sweetened condensed milk. After removing cake from oven use a skewer or fork to poke holes into the top of the cake pour caramel mixture over cake crush candy bars and sprinkle half of them over warm cake, chill. Stir cream cheese and cool whip together until blended well spread over cake, sprinkle rest of candy bar over the top.

Aunt Gracie Poor Man's Cake

Jeannie Best

1.c brown sugar
⅔ c. Crisco
1 c. water
1 c. raisins
1 tsp. cinnamon
½ tsp. nutmeg
½ soda
1 Tbsp. hot water
2 c. sifted flour
Pinch salt
½ c. nuts

Boil for 3min.cool –add tsp. soda dissolve, in Tbsp. add 2c. sifted flour
and pinch of salt add ½ c. nuts. Bake 30 min. for 1 layer or 60 min. for
loaf.

Cheesecake

Genie Thompson

___filling__
1 pkg. lemon Jell-O
1 c. boiling water
1 8oz pkg. cream cheese
½ c. sugar
1 tsp. vanilla
1 c. chilled melnot
Whipped cream

___Crust_____
½ lb. graham cracker crumbs
¼ c. melted butter.

Dissolve Jell-O in water- cool cream cheese and vanilla and sugar add Jell-O and mix well fold in whipped cream into filling.

Mix graham crackers and butter pat into a pie tin and pour filling into tin chill in refried till set.

Banana Split Cake   Al Miller

2 c. graham cracker crumbs
3 stick butter
½ c. pecans
2 c. powdered sugar
1 sm. Jar maraschino cherries
3 – 4 bananas
2 eggs
1 tsp. vanilla
1 lg. can crush pineapple drained.
10 oz. cool whip

Mix 2 c. graham cracker crumbs and 1 stick butter pat in to 9 x 13 pan, cream 2 eggs, 2 sticks butter 2 c. powder sugar, 1 tsp. vanilla beat by hand 15 min.

Spread over graham cracker bottom, slice bananas then layer, mixture, bananas, pineapple, spread cool whip over top and sprinkle with cherries and nuts.

Apricot Awesomeness

Belinda Wallis

2 pkg. crescent rolls
2 pkg. cream cheese
2 sticks butter
1 c. sugar
1 jar apricot preserves

Melt butter and pour half into bottom of 9 x 13 baking dish. Mix cream cheese and sugar together spread over crescent rolls heat apricot preserve in microwave for a few seconds to make it spreadable and spread over cream cheese place 2nd pkg. crescent rolls top and pour remaining butter over entire dish. Bake on 350 for 30 min.

Pina Colada Cake

Margaret Ralls

1 box yellow cake mix.
1 can eagle brand milk.
1 can Pina colada mix
1 bowl cool whip
½ c. coconut
½ c. pecans

Bake a yellow cake according to the box directions.

While cake is hot, make holes in cake with fork pour 1 can eagle brand milk and 1 can Pina colada mix over cake. cool top with cool whip sprinkle with coconut and pecans.

Chocolate Pie

Linda Crownover

1 c. sugar
1 heaping Tbsp. cornstarch
3 Tbsp. cocoa
1 ½ c. milk
2 eggs separated.
Butter the size of egg.
Vanilla
1 baked 8 in. pie shell

Dissolve sugar, cornstarch, and cocoa in one cup milk. Mix egg yolk, ½ c. milk, and butter. Add to first mixture, beat well and cook until thick as mush. Flavor with vanilla pour into baked crust and cover with meringue if you chose.

The Impossible Pie

Battie Schumacher

1 c. sugar
2 c. milk
1 c. coconut
½ c. flour
½ tsp. baking powder
1 ½ tsp. vanilla
2 Tbsp. butter
Pinch salt

Put all ingredients in blender put or beat with eggbeater. Pour into 10 in. pan unlined because it will make its own crust and top bake at 350 until knife comes out clean.

Cheesecake

Reva Hensley

3 oz. lemon Jell-O
1 c. boiling water
3 c. graham cracker crumbs
½ c, melted butter.
8 oz. cream cheese
1 c. sugar
1 tsp. vanilla
13 oz. stiffly whipped melnot

Dissolve pkg. lemon Jell-O in boiling water mix graham cracker crumbs and melted butter. Line bottom and sides of 9 x 13x 2 baking dish, reserve some crumbs.

Cream together pkg. cream cheese, sugar, vanilla, fold in to can stiffly whipped melnot pour into pan.

Chocolate Delight Cake

Reva Hensley

---Crust---
1 ½ c. Flour
1 ½ sticks butter.
⅔ c. pecans

---Middle----
1 c. confectioner sugar
1 pkg. cream cheese

---Top---
2 boxes chocolate pudding
3 c. milk
2 tsp. vanilla
1 bowl cool whip pecans

Crust- mix flour, butter, pecans together and press in 9 x 13 pan bake 20 to 25 min. at 350 cool. Spread cream cheese mix on crust. Mix chocolate pudding mix with milk and vanilla let it set up then pour over cheese mixture. Then put lg. container of cool whip and sprinkle with pecans.

Chocolate Carmel Cake

1 box devil food cake mix.
10 oz. diet coke
1 egg white
6 oz. fat free Carmel flavored syrup (ice cream topping)
1 c. heath candy bar chip divided.
4 oz fat free sweetened condensed milk
8 oz. fat free cool whip

Mix cake mix, egg white, and diet coke by hand- bake in 9 x 13 in. pan. Mix Carmel topping and condensed milk mix heat in microwave 2 min. when cake is done take out of oven and poke holes in it pour Carmel mix. Over hot cake then sprinkles heath chips on cake, cool cover with Kool whip and heath chips over cake.

Easy Pineapple Pie

Debbie Morrison

3.4oz. box instant vanilla pudding

14 oz. regular Borden

Eagle brand sweetened condensed milk.

2 lg. lemons

25 oz. can crush pineapple.

Premade graham cracker pie crust

8oz.original cool whip topping

In lg. bowl prepare vanilla pudding according to package directions. Pour in Borden milk into pudding. Squeeze the 2 lemons, strain and add to pudding in mixture. Drain the can of crushed pineapple and the mixture and stir until ingredients are well mixed pour into the graham cracker pie crust, top with remaining cool whip and chill at least 3 hrs. before serving.

Peanut Butter Cake

Margaret Tolleson

Cake:
½ c. Crisco
⅓ c. peanut butter
1 ½ c. brown sugar
1 tsp. vanilla
3 well beaten eggs
1 ¾ c. flour
3 ¼ tsp. baking powder
½ tsp. salt
1 ¼ c. sweet milk

Icing:
¼ c. brown sugar
¾ c. white sugar
½ c. cream (pet coronation or melnot
½ tsp. vanilla
⅓ c. peanut butter

Cake:
Bake in 2 large layer cake pans bake at 350 for 25 to 30 min. or till golden brown.

Icing:
Heat and boil for 2 min. stirring constantly. Add vanilla and peanut butter.

Beat until creamy. (you might need to add more to taste)

Mayonnaise Cake

Linda Driggers

1 c. mayonnaise
1 c. sugar
2 c. flour
2 tsp. soda
1 tsp. vanilla
½ c. cocoa
1c. boiling water

Pour boiling water over mayonnaise in large bowl mix until mayonnaise is melted. Add sugar and vanilla mix well add flour and cocoa. Add soda last to mixture will foam when soda is added. Grease and flour pan bake 40 min in a 350 oven leave out to cocoa for alight cake good for cupcakes.

Angel Pie

Margret Ralls

1 c. Cherries
1 c. Sugar
¼ c. Corn starch
1 c. pineapple tidbits
1 box orange Jell-O
4 lg. bananas
2 baked pie shells
2 c. cool whip
1 c. whipping cream

Mix cherries and a few drops of red food coloring. Mix sugar and corn starch stirring pineapple and cook on low heat until clear and slightly thick. Pour in Jell-O, dissolved and cherries and chill then add bananas Top waxed cool whip and whipping cream.

Apple Blossom Cake   Ouida Boyd

1 ½ c. cooking oil
2 c. sugar
2 eggs
3 c. flour
½ tsp. cinnamon
¼ tsp. soda
½ tsp. nutmeg
1 tsp. salt
4 c. apples chopped fine.

Mix ingredients in order listed alternating dry and apples till all mixed. bake about 1 ½ hrs. in tube pan at 350. freezes well or stays fresh in refrigerator well wrapped about 2 weeks.

Peanut Butter Delight Cake

Reva Hensley

Chocolate delight cake mix.
1 box Vanilla pudding mix
2 Tbsp. peanut butter

Mix cake from recipe or box mix light it says to, put vanilla pudding between layers of cake add peanut to pudding before putting on cake.

274

Floaty Cake

Al Miller

1 box cake mix (your choice)
1 can fruit pie filling (your choice)
2 ½ c. miniature marsh mallows

Pre-heat oven to 350, spray pans, so cake want stick. Arrange 2 ½ c. marshmallows on the bottom of the pans. mix your favorite flavor cake mix according to directions, pour over marshmallows covering them all. Then drop pie filling over the top of the cake mix. bake at 350 for 40 – 50 min or till knife comes out clean. Or center of cake does not jiggle. Some ovens my need be at 375.

Marshmallows float to the top of cake and pie filling goes to bottom.

Millionaire Pie

Carolyn Duncan

Filling:
1 lg. egg
¼ tsp. vanilla
¼ stick of butter.
3 oz. pkg. cream cheese
Baked pie shell
⅛ tsp. salt
1 c. powder sugar

Combine all ingredients, whip until creamy pour into pie shell and chill overnight.

Topping:
½ pint whipping cream.
Sugar
Pineapple crushed.
½ c. pecans

The next day, whip topping ingredients to taste, drain pineapples and add pecans cover top with them and chill again.

Fruit Cobbler

Froy Wilde

1 c. flour
1 tsp. baking powder
½ c. milk
1 c. sugar
½ tsp. salt
2 Tbsp. butter
2 c. black berries
½ c. water
1 c. sugar

Mix dry ingredients add milk and butter. Pour in buttered pan and smooth out.

Cook till burnies boil then pour over batter bake at 350 degrees. Tell butter comes to top and browns about 40 min.

Use any fruit you like.

Dewberry Cobbler

Marth Pannell

6 c. dewberries
2 c. sugar
4 Tbsp. flour
4 Tbsp. lemon juice
¼ tsp. salt

In a lg. bowl mix all ingredients line 2 qt. pans with pastry, add filling cover with top crust.

Bake in heat oven 450 for 10 min. reduce heat to 350 for 25 to 30 min. until crust is lightly browned.

Jefferson Davis Pie

Margaret Tolleson

3 c. sugar
1 c. butter
1 Tbsp. flour
1 tsp. pure vanilla
¼ tsp. salt
4 eggs lightly beaten.
1 c. milk

Cream sugar and butter blend flour, salt and vanilla into mixture and beat well add eggs than stir milk into mixture line 2-9" pie pans with pie crusts. Pour in the filling bake in 450 oven for 10 min. then reduce heat to 350 for another 30 min. or until filling is firm.

Hostess Chocolate Cake

Margaret Ralls

Filling:
¼ lb. margarine
½ c. Crisco
1 c. sugar
¾ c. pet milk
1 Tbsp. vanilla

Icing:
1 stick butter
4 Tbsp. cocoa
6 Tbsp. milk
1 tsp. vanilla
1 box powder sugar
1 tsp. vanilla

Bake your favorite chocolate cake in 3 layers, cool.

Filling:
Beat 8 – 10 min. until light and fluffy spread between layers.

Icing:
Bring to a boil, remove from heat, add a box powder sugar, vanilla beat well.

Pineapple Sheet Cake

Vernice Boyd

2 c. sugar
½ c. veg. oil
2 eggs
1 c. (15 ½ oz.) crushed pineapple
2 tsp. baking soda
2 c. flour
⅛ tsp. salt

Icing:
1 stick (½ C.) Butter
1 c. sugar
1 sm. Can carnation evaporated milk
1 c. coconut
1 c. pecans

Mix all ingredients, pour onto cookie sheet or oblong pan. Bake 45 min. at 350 while cake is cooking, make icing.

Icing:
Boil butter, sugar and milk until melted and bubbly add coconut and nuts. Pour over cake while still hot.

Coconut — Pecan Filling and Frosting
Nellie Tuck

1 can(12 oz.) evaporated milk
1 ½ C. Sugar
¾ c.(1 ½ sticks) butter
4 egg yolks, slightly beaten.
1 ½ tsp. vanilla
1 pkg. coconut flakes (about 2 ⅓ c.)
1 ½ c. pecans

Stir milk, butter, egg yolks, and vanilla in lg. saucepan. stirring constantly, cook on med. heat 12 mins. Or until thickened and golden brown. Remove from heat.

Stir in coconut and pecans. Cool to room temperature and spreading consistency.

German Chocolate Cake

Nellie Tuck

4 oz. sweet (German) chocolate coarsely chopped.
½ c. boiling water
2 tsp. vanilla
2 ½ c. sifted cake flour or 2 c. all-purpose flour
1 tsp. baking soda
1 tsp. salt
1 c. butter or oil, softened.
2 c. sugar or 1 c. sugar and 1 c. packed brown sugar
4 lg. egg yolks
1 c. butter milk or (milk and 1 Tbsp. white vinegar or 1 Tbsp. lemon juice to equal 1 c.)
4 lg. egg whites

Pre heat oven to 350. Grease and dust with flour 2- 8 x 2 round cake pans or spray with pan spray.

Put chocolate in med bowl pour boiling water over top and stir till melted. Let cool add vanilla.

Sift together the dry ingredients.in lg. bowl beat butter until smooth add sugar beat until smooth the eggs mixing well the pour in the chocolate. Mixing well. Then add the dry ingredients slowly mixing and alternately with the milk as you do. Mixing till smooth. The batter will be thick.

In med. bowl beat the egg whites until stiff. When done fold half into the cake mix. Mix well the add rest of the egg whites and mix in till smooth.

Divide mix into the pans equally and bake 45 to 50 mins. Or till toothpick comes out clean when checked the cake.

Let cool then put on cake plate and frost.

Death by Decadents
Loria Flynn

2 boxes of brownies
1 bag small marshmallows
1 lb. bag simi sweet chocolate chips
1lb bag caramels

In med bowl mix brownie mix according to instructions on bag.

Pour half in bottom of a ready cake pan, put candy and marshmallows on top of that and put other half of mix on top of the candy. put in the oven and cook tell brownies are done. Serve worm or cold and can serve with ice cream.

Orange Cake
Nellie Tuck

1 ½ c. Phills berry's best flour
6 Tbsp. butter
1 c. sugar
1 tsp. baking powder
2 eggs
½ c. milk
1 tsp. Orange extract

Cream butter and sugar slowly sift the baking powder with the flour add 1 Tbsp. mixture to the butter and sugar add eggs mix till smooth continuing adding flour and milk alternately until both are used flavor with orange extract bake about 35 mins. At 350 until toothpick comes clean when checking the cake.

Orange Frosting

Nellie Tuck

1 egg yolk
½ tsp. orange extract
1 Tbsp. Water
Confectioners' sugar

Mix first 3 ingredients and add enough sugar to make frosting of right consistency to spread.

For 1 cake for 2-layer double recipe.

Loria's Chocolate Graham Torte
Loria Flynn

4 eggs
1lbs. (5 ¼ c.) crushed chocolate graham crackers
2 c. sugar
1 c. butter
4 tsp. baking powder

Pre heat oven to 350. Combine crackers and baking soda, set aside. In lg. bowl cream butter and sugar. Add eggs milk and crackers mix till well blended.

Pour into ungreased 9 x 13 in. pan cook for 45 to 50 mins. Cool

Chocolate Frosting
Loria Flynn

½ butter
¼ c. cocoa
6 Tbsp. milk
1 box powdered sugar
1 tsp. vanilla

Combine and cook to boiling, butter cocoa, and milk. Remove from heat add powdered sugar and vanilla add chopped nuts if you like.

Cream Cheese Icing
Loria Flynn

1 c. butter
1 box cream cheese
1 box powdered sugar
1 tsp. vanilla
¼ c. milk

Cream together butter and cream cheese and milk till smooth then add sugar and vanilla till smooth.

Chocolate Velvet Frosting

Loria Flynn

1 bag simi sweet chocolate chips
3 Tbsp. butter
¼ c. milk
1 tsp. vanilla
¼ tsp. salt
3 c. powdered sugar

Melt chocolate chips and butter over hot not boiling water. Remove from heat add milk, vanilla and salt mix until well blended beat in sugar gradually till smooth.

Grandma Sarah's Apple Brown
Bettye Sarah Morrison

10 to 12 apples peeled and cored and sliced.
2 tsp. cinnamon
1 ¼ c. flour
¾ c. brown sugar
¼ lb. butter

Syrup:
⅔ c. brown sugar
¼ c. hot water
½ juice of a lemon

Preheat oven to 350. Arrange slices in the bottom of a lightly greased 12 x 9 pan.

Sprinkle with cinnamon. Mix flour and brown sugar cut in butter until crumbly and set aside.

Combine syrup ingredients and stir well drizzle over mixture of apples. Cover with flour mixture pour remaining syrup over top bake 350 for 1 hr.

THIS & THAT

Raised Doughnuts

Juanita Carlile

1 c. milk
¾ c. sugar
¼ c. warm water
1 pkg. yeast
4 ½ c. flour
¼ c. shortening.
½ tsp. salt
2 eggs

Scold milks add ¼ c. sugar, let cool to luck warm. Measure water into small bowl. Add yeast and stir until dissolved, add to milk add 2 flour and beat until smooth. Cover and let rise in warm place until doubled in size. Cream shorting and remaining sugar stir in eggs and salt. Stir this into yeast mix then stir in remaining flour place in greased bowl, cover and let rise about 40 mins. Or until double in size. Turn out on floured board and roll out to about ⅓ in" thick cut with doughnut cutter place on floured board. Cover with cloth, let rise until double drop into 370 deep fat fryer raised side down cook 2- or 3-min. turn only while still warm dip in sugar or glazed as follows.

Confectioner Glaze

Juanita Carlile

1 c. confectioner sugar
¼ c. boiling water
½ tsp. vanilla

Mix 1 c. confectioner sugar with ¼ c. boiling water. Bring to boil stir in ½ tsp. vanilla 1 c. warm glaze 2 dozen doughnuts.

Caramel Popcorn

Linda Crownover

2 batches of popcorn –butter
1 stick butter
1 c. brown sugar
½ c. Karo

Place 2 batches of popped corn in a butter roaster pan.in a saucepan, boiling for 5 mins. 1 stick butter,1 c. brown sugar, pour the sugar mixture over the popcorn and stir well. Then add ½ c. Karo, stirring well as you pour. Bake in 250 oven for 45 min. to 1 hr. stir evenly.

Ham and Cheese Breakfast Quiche

Al Miller

30 oz. pkg. frozen hash brown potatoes
⅓ c. butter, melted.
1 ½ c. cooked diced ham or sausage
1 ½ c. shredded monetary jack cheese.
6 eggs
½ c. half & half

Preheat oven to 425 defrost potatoes. Squeeze out any excess moisture from the potatoes and combine them with the melted butter in a small bowl press this mixture into the bottom and sides of an ungreased 9 x 13 pan.

Cake at 425 for 25 min. edges should be a bit brown can be refrigerated overnight and recipe completed the next morning.

Remove pan from oven and arrange the ham and cheese evenly over the potatoes. In a separate bowl, beat together eggs and half & half. pour this over the ham and cheese. Return pan to oven and bake 425 from 30 mins. Or until the liquid has completely set.

Strawberry Preserves
Loria Flynn via Nelly Tuck

2 qts. Strawberries
Boiling water
2 pint's sugar
1 pint's sugar

2 qts. Strawberries cover with water boil for 1 min. drain off water add 2 pints sugar boil 3 mins. Take off heat, add 1–pint sugar boil 3 mins. When cold put in jars.

Lemon Sauce

1 stick butter
1 c. sugar
¼ tsp. salt
½ c. light corn syrup
1 c. pet milk
½ c. lemon juice

Melt butter, add sugar, salt, and syrup. Cook over low heat stirring constantly for 3 – 4 mins. Remove from heat and stir in milk slow. Add lemon juice and beat extremely hard and good.

Ice Cream

Reva Hensley via Joyce Sulpkeer

1 can eagle Brand cream.
1 ¾ c. sugar
½ tsp. salt
2 tsp. vanilla
4 lg. eggs

Beat 5 – 10 mins., pet in freezer and fill with homo milk mix as ice cream mixer says to.

4 – pie crust

Al miller

3 c. flour
1 tsp. salt
1 Tbsp. sugar
1 ¼ c. Crisco
1 egg
1 Tbsp. vinegar
5 Tbsp. water

Place in lg. Tupperware bowl blend by shaping. beat egg, vinegar, water, shake until it forms a ball ready to roll out.

Pop Corn Ball

3 qts. Popcorn (popped)
1 c. sugar
⅓ c. white syrup
⅓ c. water
¼ c. butter
¾ tsp. salt
¾ tsp. vanilla

Mix sugar, syrup, water, butter, salt in saucepan and cook string until the sugar is dissolved. continue cooking without stirring until syrup forms a brittle ball in cold water or 300 on candy thermometer add vanilla and stir only enough to mix it. Put popcorn in greased buttered lg. bowl pour syrup over it mix with buttered hands.

Popsicles

2 c. boiling water
1 pkg. Kool-Aid
3 oz. pkg. Jell-O
1 c. sugar

Mix until dissolved then add 2 c. cold water.

Half Recipes — Popsicles
Nancy P. Burnett

1 c. boiling water 1 tsp. Kool- Aid
¼ c. Jell–O
½ c. sugar

Dissolve and add 1 c. cold water.

Orange Pear Jell-O

Alberta Kennedy

1 c. pears
½ c. sugar
6 cinnamon sticks
2 boxes orange Jell-O
2 ½ c. boiling water

Drain juice from a can of pears. Boil juice and about ½ c. of sugar and cinnamon sticks. let boil for 2 mins. Then add pears bring to a boil again. Chill overnight.

Dissolve 2 boxes orange Jell-O with 2 ½ c. boiling water. Add the chilled mixture and enough water to make a cup arrange pear halves in a mold. Serve with cool whip.

Crust

Martha Pannell

2 c. flour
1 tsp. salt
⅔ c. shortening

Mix until like corn meal then add 6 to 8 Tbsp. one at a time of water.

Chill dough divide dough ⅔ for bottom and ⅓ for top.

Roll out put in pie pan cook in oven till brown or to taste.

Chocolate Ice Cream
Linda Crownover

6 eggs
3 c. sugar
6 Tbsp. vanilla
½ tsp. salt
1 lg. can carnation milk
1 box chocolate instant pudding
1 qt. half & half

Mix all ingredients well then fill with whole milk. freeze in ice cream freezer as directed.

Meringa

Linda Crownover

2 egg whites
¼ tsp. cream of tarter
⅓ c. sugar

2 egg whites and ¼ tsp. cream of tartar, beat until frothy, add ⅓ c. sugar by tbsp. at a time until it stains at stiff pick by beating the hole time after each tbsp. of sugar, put on pie and brown in oven.

Orange Jell-O

Jennie Best

1 lg. pkg. orange Jell-O
1 sm. Can froze orange juice.
1 can pineapple chucks
1 can Mandurian oranges

Dissolve Jell-O in 2 c. boiling water. Add orange juice concentrate. then fruit chill until sets up.

Never Fail Pie Crust

Reba Quetone

3 c. flour
1 tsp. salt
1 c. & 2 Tbsp. shortening
1 egg
5 Tbsp. water
1 tsp. vinegar

Mix, cut shortening into flour and salt. Add liquid mixture. Divide into 2 balls roll on floured surface.

Strawberry Frozen Dessert

Martha Pannell

1 pt. whipping cream
2 ½ c. powdered sugar (1 box)
½ lb. butter
5 eggs
4 – 10 oz. frozen strawberries
Cookie crumbs

Cream sugar and butter together beat eggs slightly and blend add strawberries and nuts whip cream and fold in. chill line bottom of pan with half of the cookie crumbs top with more crumbs freeze at least 24 hrs.

Three Ice Cream
Reva Hensley

3 c. sugar
3 oranges
3 c. half & half
3 lemons
3 c. milk
3 bananas

Blend sugar, half & half, milk stir until sugar is dissolved. Place in ice cream maker and turn until nearly frozen. Remove lid and pour in the juice of lemons, oranges and pealed bananas pulverized in a blender, continue freezing until ready to pack.

Quick Pineapple Jell-O   Carolyn Duncan

Can of pineapple
Sm. box of Jell-O
Boiling water

Open end of can of sliced pineapple do not empty pineapple -leave in can using small box of Jell-O mix using half amount of water, pour Jell-O into can and let set, open another end to release it slice it and serve with cottage cheese or alone.

COOKIES & CANDY

No Bake Cookies

3 c oats

3 c. sugar

¼ c. milk

¼ c. Hershey cocoa

1 c. peanut butter

¼ c. melted butter.

1 tsp. vanilla

Mix all ingredients until well blended drop by spoon full on cookie sheet put in fried to set up.

One Pan Brownies

Martha Pannell

1 stick butter
2 oz. unsweetened chocolate
1 c. sugar
1 c. unbroken pecans
½ c. flour
1 tsp. baking powder
1 tsp. vanilla
2 eggs

In a 9 x 9 in" pan, melt butter with unsweetened chocolate in the oven remove, pecans, flour, baking powder, and vanilla. Mix to blend add eggs and stir. Bake at 350 for 30 min. cool and cut into squares.

4 Dozen Brownies

Margaret Ralls

Brownies:
1 c. 2 Tbsp. butter
2 ¼ c. sugar
2 tsp. vanilla
1 c. nuts chopped.
⅔ c. cocoa
5 eggs, beaten.
¾ c. flour

Icing:
1 stick butter
1 egg
1 tsp. vanilla
1 box powdered sugar
½ c. cocoa

Melt butter in another bowl beat eggs then add sugar, vanilla 3 mins. add butter and enough cold coffee to make it spreadable.

Flour, cocoa, and nuts. Pour into lg. 11 x 9 in" pan bake at 325 for 20 -25 min. be sure and don't over bake. Then ice while hot with this icing.

Blackberry Pie Bars

Al Miller

Crust:
3 c. all - purpose flour
1 ½ c. sugar
¼ tsp. salt
1 ½ c. (3 sticks) unsalted butter, chilled
Fruit filling:
4 lg. eggs
2 c. sugar
1 c. sour cream
¾ c. flour
Pinch salt
Zest of ½ lemon
1 tsp. almond extract
2 (16 oz.) packages frozen black berries thawed and drained canned is best

Pre heat oven to 350 greased a 9 x 13 baking pan.

Crust: combine flour, sugar and salt in the bowl of a processor. Pulse a few times to mix. Cut distributed but the mixture is still crumbly 30 – 6- sec. the

Filling:

Preserve 1 ½ c. of mixture for the top press the rest into the bottom of pan and bake 12 – 15 mins. Cool at least 10 mins.

To make the filling, whisk the eggs in a lg. bowl then add the sugar, sour cream, flour, salt, lemon zest, and almonds extract, gently fold in the berries and spoon the mixture over curst. sprinkle the top crust evenly over the filling and bake 45 – 55 mins. Cool at least 1 hr., before cutting into bars or scoop out of the pan to serve cobbler style.

German Chocolate Carmel Bars

Genie Thompson

Melt:
60 light camels
½ c. evaporated milk
1 pkg. German chocolate cake mix.
⅓ c. evaporated milk
¾ c. melted butter.
1 c. nuts(chopped)

Spread ½ cake mixture in a greased and floured 9 x 13 baking pan bake 8 min. at 350.

Sprinkle 1 c. chocolate chips over this, then pour caramel mix over this.

Crumble remaining cake mix over top of this, bake 18 – 20 min. at 350 cool slightly and refrigerate at least 30 mins. To set caramels.

Pecan Bars

Carolyn Duncan

2 c. flour
1 c. sugar
1 tsp. soda
1 tsp. cinnamon
½ tsp. salt
1 c. nuts
1 egg, beaten.
¾ c. oil
¼ c. honey

Icing:
1 c. powdered sugar
2 Tbsp. mayonnaise
1 Tbsp water

Sift above ingredients, then add flour, sugar, cinnamon, salt, soda, nuts add beaten egg, honey, oil, mix and put in jelly roll pan this is very thick and will have to be patted down. Bake at 350 for 12 mins.

While cooking mix powdered sugar, mayo, and water then ice cake with it and roll up if can.

Coconut toffee Bars

Barbara Anderson

½ c. shortening.
1 c. brown sugar
1 c. flour
2 eggs
1 c. brown sugar
1 tsp. vanilla
½ tsp. salt
2 tsp. flour
1 c. coconut
1 c. chopped nuts.

Mix and press into bottom of 9 x 13 in" pan bake 10 min. at 350.

Beat 2 eggs add 1 c. baking powder,1 tsp. vanilla,½ tsp. salt, 2 c. flour,1 c. coconut,1 c. chopped pour over cake and put back in oven return to oven bake 25 mins. Cooled slightly cut into bars.

Twix Bars
Carroll Ann Tolleson

Original club crackers
1 c. graham crackers, crushed.
¾ c. brown sugar
½ c. white sugar
⅓ c. milk
½ c. butter
⅔ c. peanut butter
1 c. butter scotch or semi- sweet chocolate chips

Place 1 layer of original club crackers on the bottom of a greased 9 x 13"

pan. in a lg. saucepan over low heat, combine graham crackers crumbs, brown sugar, white sugar, milk, and butter. Stir together and boil for 5 mins. pour mixture into pan over crackers cover with and other layer of crackers. In microwave or double boiler, melt peanut butter and butter scotch or chocolate chips, stirring often until smooth pour over top of crackers and let cool some cover and refrigerate till firm and cut into bars.

Cowboy Cookie Haze

Margaret Ralls

2 c. flour
1 tsp. soda
½ tsp. salt
½ tsp. baking powder
1 c. shortening
1 c. white sugar
1 c. brown sugar
1 tsp. vanilla
1 pkg. chocolate chips
2 eggs
2 c. oatmeal

Sift flour, soda, salt, baking powder together, blend shortening, sugar and eggs together until light and fluffy. Add flour mix to oil mix. Add oats, vanilla, and chips and nuts if desired. Bake in 350 oven for 15 min.

Chocolate Snappers

Margaret Ralls

1 pkg. milk chocolate cake mix.
⅔ c. shortening
2 eggs
2 ½ c. pecans halves
1 tub creamy chocolate frosting

Heat oven to 375 beat about half of cake mix dry, the shortening and eggs in lg. bowl at med. Speed until smooth. Stir in remaining cake mix. For each cookie place 3 pecan halves on ungreased cookie sheet, place 1 tsp. Dough in center of each group of pecans.

Baking 8 to 10 min. or until center are slightly puffed and edges are set. Cool completely, remove from cookie sheet and frost with frosting.

Reese Cups

Linda Crownover

1 qt. peanut butter
1 lb. butter, soften.
2 boxes powder sugar
1 slice paraffin
3 (6oz.) pkgs. Chocolate chips

Mix butter, peanut butter, and powder sugar roll into balls.

Melt chocolate and paraffin together. Dip balls in chocolate put on wax paper till all done and let set when dry there ready to eat.

Peanut Brittle

Margaret Ralls

1 c. sugar
1 c. raw peanuts
½ c. light corn syrup
1 tsp. vanilla
1 tsp. butter
1 tsp. soda

Cook 4 min on high in microwave, stir mixture after 2 ½ min. cook longer, stir in vanilla, butter, cook 1 min. longer, stir in soda fast. pour on to buttered pan. let set. Cook in Glass bowl

Instant Pudding Cookies

Carolyn Duncan

¾ c. Bisquick
¼ c. salad oil
1 egg
3 ¾ oz. pkg. instant pudding any flavor

Mix ingredients well, form into balls press Criss cross with floured fork bake 8 – 10 min. at 350 makes 2 doz.

Mosaic cookies (no-bake)

Pat Hauser

6 oz. chocolate chip
2 Tbsp. butter
1 c. powder sugar
¼ tsp. butter flavoring
½ tsp. sugar flavoring
1 c. chopped nuts.
4 c.-colored marshmallows
Graham crackers
Coconut

Melt chocolate chips and butter together over warm water in double broiler. remove from heat and add egg, sugar, flavorings, nuts and marshmallows. For into rolls 2 in." long roll in graham cracker crumbs and coconut

Nut squares

Reva Hensley Via Her Mom

2 c. sugar
2 c. coarsely chopped nuts
2 eggs
1 c. flour

Mix well put on a lined cookie sheet, Bake 20 – 25 mins. In med. Oven about 350 8 – 10 min.

let cool and cut in squares. Do not overcook.

Strawberry Cream Squares   Nancy Matson Via Reva Hensley

6 oz. pkg. strawberry Jell-O
2 c. boiling water
20 oz frozen strawberries
13 ½ oz. can crushed pineapple.
2 lg. ripe bananas
1 c. dairy sour cream

Dissolve Jell-O in boiling water, add frozen strawberries, stir occasionally till thawed. Add crushed pineapple, and diced banana. Pour half in to 8 x 8 x8 2 in." pan chill ½ firm spread evenly with 1 c. sour cream pour remaining Jell-O on top. chill till firm. Cut into squares top with sour cream dollops.

Peanut Butter Creams

Margaret Ralls via Margaret Moore

1 box powder sugar
1 ½ c. peanut butter
⅓ c. milk
¼ c. honey
½ tsp. salt
1 tsp. vanilla
6 oz pkg. chocolate chips – for top

Combine all the above until well blended. Pour into 9 x 13 glass cake pan melt 6 oz. chocolate chips pour over peanut butter mixture, chill.

Peanut Butter Logs

Linda Crownover

1 c. peanut Butter
2 Tbsp. butter
1 ½ c. powder sugar
3 c. crisp rice cereal
Chopped peanuts, optional.

In a bowl blend together peanut butter and butter, stir in powder sugar. Add rice cereal, mixing well shape into 3 logs. Pat peanuts over logs wrap in foil or plastic wrap and chill.

Lemon Bars

Genie Thompson

1 c. butter, softened.
2 ¼ c. flour, divided.
½ c. powdered sugar
4 eggs, battened.
2 c. sugar
½ c. lemon juice
Dash of salt
1 tsp. baking powder
Powdered sugar

Combine butter, flour, and powder sugar, blend until smooth.

Pat dough into a lightly greased 13 x 9 x 2 in." pan bake at 350 for 30 mins.

Combine eggs, sugar, and lemon juice mix well add flour, salt, and baking powder, blend well. Pour over pastry. Bake at 300 for 30 to 40 mins. Or until done. Sprinkle well with powdered sugar and cut into large squares.

Christmas Cookies

Nancy P. Burnett

1 c. soften butter.
1 ½ c. sugar
1 egg
1 tsp. vanilla
1 tsp. almond extract
2 ½ c. self-rising flour

Mix butter, sugar, eggs, vanilla and almond extract well. Blend in flour, cover and chill 3 hrs. roll dough out to ¼ to ½ in" thick on floured board. Cut with cookie cutters bake in 375 oven on greased cookie sheet for 7 – 8 mins. Or till golden brown on edges.

Brown — Eyed Susan's

Linda Crownover

1 c. butter
3 Tbsp. Sugar
1 tsp. vanilla
2 c. flour
½ tsp. salt

Cream butters add remaining ingredients shape into balls one inch wide and flatten with you thumb on cookie sheet bake in 400 oven 10 to 12 min. when cool, frost.

Frosting:
1 c. powdered sugar
2 Tbsp. cocoa
2 Tbsp. hot water
½ tsp. vanilla
Mix well place ½ tsp. in the thumbprint of each cookie.

Brownie

Froy Wilde

½ c. butter
1 c. sugar
2 eggs slightly beaten.
1 tsp. vanilla
⅔ c. flour
⅔ c. chop nuts
6 Tbsp. cocoa

Mix all ingredients together until just mixed lightly, bake in square cake pan 25 min. at 325 do not over bake.

Linda's Fudge

Linda Driggers

4 c. sugar

1 lb. can pet milk.

½ lb. butter

3 (6 oz.) pks. Chocolate chips

24 lg. marshmallows

1 c. nuts(if desired)

1 tsp. vanilla

Boil sugar and milk 10 mins. (no longer) last 2 mins. Add butter. Remove from stove, add chocolate chips and stir add marshmallows add vanilla and nuts stir and pour into buttered 9 x 13" pan.

Evelyn's Divinity

2 ½ c. white sugar
½ c. white corn syrup
½ c. cold water
2 egg whites
1 c. nut(if desired)
1 tsp. vanilla

Cook first 3 ingredients to 250; pour over stiffly beaten egg whites. Cook rest of syrup to 263. Pour into egg mixture add vanilla. beat until it starts to loss gloss; add nuts drop by spoon full onto wax paper or put in butter lines square pan.

Southern Tea Cakes

Loria Flynn

1 c. butter, softened.
2 c. sugar
3 lg. eggs
1 tsp. vanilla
3 ½ c. all-purpose flour
1tsp. baking powder
½ tsp. salt

Beat butter at med. speed with an electric mixer until cream; gradually.

Add sugar. Beat add eggs one at a time, beating after each addition. Add vanilla, beat until blended. Add flour, salt and soda to butter mixture, beat at low speed. Divide dough in half; wrap each portion in plastic wrap and chill 1 hr. roll half of dough to ¼ inch. Thickness on a floured surface cut out cookie shapes place on cookie sheet on wax paper bake at 350. For 10 to 12 mins. Or until edges begin to brown, let stand on sheet to cool.

Chocolate Chip Cookies

Loria Flynn

3 ¼ c. all-purpose flour
1 tsp. baking soda
½ tsp. salt
1 c. butter, melted.
1c. brown sugar packed.
2 tsp. vanilla
2 eggs
1 c. white sugar
2 c. chocolate chips

Pre-heat oven to 350. in lg. bowl combine butter, sugar vanilla and eggs beat until creamy. mix in flour, salt, and soda. Gradually mix in flour mix with butter mix and combine thoroughly then fold in chips. Drop on cookie sheet and bake till golden brown 8 to 10 mins.

Cave Cookies
Johnny Flynn

1 c. butter

1 c. brown sugar, packed

1 c. white sugar

2 eggs

1 tsp. vanilla

1 tsp. baking powder

1 tsp. baking soda

2 ½ c. all-purpose flour

2 ½ c. oatmeal

1 c. chocolate chips

1 c. raisins

1 c. nuts (if desired)

1 c. yogurt (if desired)

Mix all dry ingredients together and all the wet ingredients together then combine them slowly as you mix thoroughly drop by spoon full on cookie sheet bake 8 to 10 mins or golden brown.

Ginger Cookies

Linda Driggers

¾ c. butter
1 c. sugar
¼ c. molasses
1 egg
2 c. all-purpose flour
2 tsp. soda
½ tsp. salt
½ tsp. cloves
½ tsp. ginger
1 tsp. cinnamon

Cream sugar, butter until smooth then mix in molasses and egg thoroughly mixed. then sift dry ingredients together in another bowl then slowly stir in with the butter mix a little at a time. Chill if you want to for 1 hr. if you want to, so its easier to work with. Form dough into 1 in. balls and bake at 350 for 12 mins. Or till browned and flattened.

Chocolate Mexican Wedding Cookies

Linda Driggers

1 ⅔ c. all-purpose flour
1 c. pecans toasted and chopped.
⅓ c. unsweetened cocoa powder
¾ tsp. cinnamon
¼ tsp. salt
⅛ to ¼ tsp. ground cayenne
2 sticks butter, room temp.
1 ½ c. powder sugar, divided.
1 tsp. vanilla

In lg. bowl mix dry ingredients together, set aside.

In med. bowl mix butter and ½ c. powder sugar beat on med. high for 3 mins. Beat in vanilla move to low speed gradually add in the flour mixture until combined. Transfer the dough to plastic wrap. Form into a 1 in. dick wrap completely in plastic refrigerate until firm but still soft enough to scoop 45 mins. To 1 hr.

Meanwhile arrange 2 racks to divide the oven into thirds and heat to 350. Line baking sheets with parchment paper place 1 c. of powder sugar in a pie plate.

Form the dough into 1Tbsp. about 1 ¼ apart balls and place on cookie sheets. bake 8 mins. Rotate the cookie sheets from front to back bake until top of cookies are set 7-8 mins.

Cool 10 mins. While still warm coat each cookie in powder sugar. Let cool completely about 15 mins, then coat again.

Creamy Pralines

Linda Driggers

1 c. sugar
1 c. firmly packed brown sugar
1 (14 oz.) can sweetened condensed milk
¾ c. butter
½ c. light corn syrup
⅛ tsp. salt
3 c. pecan pieces
1 tsp. vanilla
½ to 1 tsp. almond extract

Grease wax paper sheet with butter, then set aside. Combine sugar and the next 5 ingredients in a lg. saucepan cook over low heat, stirring gently. until butter melts. Cook over med. heat stirring constantly, until mixture reaches soft ball stage or 238 on candy temp. Remove from heat, stir in pecans and flavorings. Beat with a wooden spoon just until mixture begins to thicken working rapidly, drop by rounded Tbsp. onto prepared wax paper. Let stand until firm.

White Chocolate Lemon Fudge
Johnny Flynn

1 c. cream
5 tsp. butter
4 tsp. lemon extract
24 oz.(3 boxes) baker's white baking chocolate
1 c. shredded coconut
1 c. powdered sugar

Break the chocolate into small pieces and put in a lg. bowl, along with the butter.

In a sm. saucepan, bring cream slowly to a light boil. Pour the boiling cream over the chocolate and keep stirring until the chocolate is melted. Beat well, as if for ganache. Add powdered sugar, lemon extract, and coconut, and pour into a 9 x 9 in. glass baking pan. Let sit for 2 hrs. or till firm.

Pretzel Turtles

Johnny Flynn

1 bag Rollo candies
1 sm. (16 oz.) bag sm., knotted pretzels
1 med. size bag (6oz.) of pecans

Lay out pretzels on ungreased cookie sheet. Put a Rollo candy on each pretzel. Put in oven at 250 for 4 mins. Take out and top each with pecan (press pecan in lightly) put in refrigerator to harden for 3 mins. (do not leaven in the refrigerator)

Pumpkin Cookies

Johnny Flynn

1 c. butter
1 c, sugar
2 c. all-purpose flour
1 tsp. baking powder
½ tsp. cinnamon
1 c. canned pumpkin
1 egg
1c.raisins
½ c. chopped walnuts or pecans.

Cream butter, pumpkin and egg together in med. bowl. Sift dry ingredients together in med. bowl. Then add to the butter mixture slowly thoroughly then fold in raisins and nuts.

Drop by spoon onto an ungreased cookie sheet bake at 350.

Combine butter, sugar, and milk in a saucepan cook over low heat stirring constantly until dissolved remove from burner and add cream cheese stir until smooth drizzle over cookies.

Oatmeal Raisin Cookies

Grace Head

2 ¼ c. all-purpose flour
½ tsp. baking soda
¼ tsp. salt
1c. oatmeal
1 c. butter, softened.
1 c. packed brown sugar
½ c. sugar
2 eggs
2 Tbsp. honey
2 tsp. vanilla
1 ½ c. raisins
½ c. nuts, chopped (if desired)

Mix all dry ingredients together. Cream butter, sugar and eggs beat
well. Stir in honey and vanilla. Add flour mixture slowly while stirring
fold in raisins and nuts. Drop by Tbsp. on ungreased cookie sheet about
2 in. apart bake at 350 for 18 to 20 mins.

Amira's Cookies

Amira Flynn

1 c. butter, softened.
1 c. packed brown sugar
1 egg
2 tsp. almond extract
1 tsp. vanilla extract
3 ½ c. all-purpose flour
¼ c. sm. chocolate chips
¼ c. Colored candies

In a bowl, cream butter and brown sugar, beat egg and extracts. sift dry ingredients together all slowly to wet ingredients mixing thoroughly then cover and chill for 1 hr. shape into balls place on ungreased cookie sheet place in a 325 oven for 12 mins. Cool before eating.

THIS AND THAT / MISCELLANEOUS

Chocolate Dipped Delights

Loria Flynn

1 pkg. 4 oz. baker's German's sweet Baking Chocolate

Melt Chocolate dip assorted fresh or dried fruit, cookies, nut's, or pretzels into chocolate, cover at least half. Let excess chocolate drip off. Let stand or refrigerate on wax paper- lined tray 30 min. or until chocolate is firm. Drizzle with melted white chocolate, if desired. Refrigerate fresh fruit in refrigerator up to 2 days. Store dried fruit, cookies, nuts and pretzels in airtight container.

Breeks liniment

Marion Wilemon

Turpentine 8 oz.
Camphor 1 oz.
Chloroform 1 oz.
Oil of Mustard 3 drams
Oil of Cinnamon 2 drams
Oil of Cedar 2 drams
Oil of Mint 2 drams
Oil of Cloves 2 drams
Gas 3 qtrs.

This will make one gallon.

Raspberry Glaze

Loria Flynn

½ c. seedless raspberry jam
1 Tbsp. fresh lime juice
2 ½ c. fresh raspberries

Melt jam in med. saucepan over low heat; stir in lime juice. Remove from heat. Add raspberries, stirring gently to combine. remove from heat and pour berry mixture through fine – wire mesh strainer into bowl, pressing with the back of a spoon. Discard solids.

Tomatillo Tartar Sauce

Loria Flynn

½ lb. tomatillos(about 8 med.)
1 c. mayo
2 tsp. lime juice
2 jalapeno peppers seeded and chopped finely.
¼ c. chopped cilantro.
1 tsp. ground cumin
½ tsp. salt

Remove husks from tomatillos and rinse well; finely chop to make 1 cup tomatillos.

Stir together tomatillos, lime juice, jalapenos, cilantro, cumin and salt.

Serve with grilled sea foods.

Chimichurri
Loria Flynn

1 c. fresh parsley finely chopped.

6 cloves garlic finely chopped.

1 tsp. fresh oregano finely chopped.

½ to 1 tsp. crushed pepper flashes (red or black)

½ c. olive oil or veg. oil.

½ c. white vinegar

1 tsp. lemon juice

Place parsley in 2 c. measuring glass, gently pressing. Add garlic, oregano and pepper flakes; stir to mix. Add oil, vinegar and lemon juice; mix well using fork. Season to taste. With salt and pepper. The chimichurri should be thick. Sauce can be refrigerated for several days. Stir before serving.

Pineapple frozen bars

Loria Flynn

2 c. chopped summer fruits(pineapple, oranges, strawberries, etc.)
1 Tbsp. sugar(optional)
1 tsp. lemon juice

Puree fruit in blender, adding a Tbsp. or 2 of water if necessary. Add sugar, if desired, and lemon juice and blend.

Pour into bar molds or small cups and insert sticks.

Freeze until solid.

Cantaloupe shaved Ice

Loria Flynn

4 c. cantaloupe(1 med. melon) or other fruit
1 (6 oz.) can froze lemonade concentrate.
1 to 2 Tbsp. powdered sugar(optional)
Sweetened coconut flakes, fresh mint leaves(optional)

Combine cantaloupe and lemonade concentrate in food processor bowl. Process until smooth. Sweeten to taste with powdered sugar, if desired.

Pour cantaloupe mixture into an 11 x 7-inch glass baking dish. Freeze 30 mins. Remove from freezer; stir mixture. Return to freezer 30 mins. more. remove and scrape mixture with fork to form shaved ice. Return to freezer. Repeat freeze/scrape process until ice is slushy but not completely frozen, about 3 to 4 hrs. spoon shaved ice into bowls or chilled dishes. Top with coconut and mint, if desired, and serve immediately.

Tiger Butter

Loria Flynn

1 pkg. white almond bark
1 c. peanut butter
1 c. chocolate chips.

Melt almond bark and peanut butter mix well. Pour on cookie sheet lined with wax paper melt chocolate chips drizzle over bark and peanut butter marble with knife cool until set.

Cherry Sauce for Ham

Margaret Ralls

1 stick cinnamon
1 tsp. whole cloves
1 ½ c. sugar
2 Tbsp. cornstarch
Salt
1 can of cherries and juice
¾ c. orange juice

Put all in saucepan on med. high and heat until thick with stirring a lot to keep from burning.

Cherry Sauce

Loria Flynn

1 stick cinnamon
1 tsp. whole cloves
1 ½ c. sugar
2 Tbsp. corn starch
1 can (16 oz.) Undrained can pitted cherries.
¾ c. orange juice
1 Tbsp. lemon juice

Add coffee filter bag of spices cook on med. heat until thick.

WW Dream Sickle Pudding
Marion Wilemon

1 bx. Instant pudding any flavor
1 can mandarin oranges drained.
1 container cool whip 8oz
1 bx. orange Jell-O
1c. Boiling water
3 Ice cubes

Dissolve Jell-O in 1 c. boiling water add 3 ice cubs to boiling water after Jell-O is dissolved cold put water to make 1 c. drain oranges and set a side for 5 mins. With electric mixer stir 1 pkg. instant pudding into Jell-O let stand 15 mins. Mix then fold in cool whip and oranges.

Homemade Taco Seasoning

Johnny Flynn

1 Tbsp. chili powder
½ tsp. chipotle pepper powder
1 tsp. cumin
1 tsp. garlic powder
1 tsp. onion powder
½ tsp. dried cilantro
1 tsp. black pepper

In a sm. bowl add all spices. Mix thoroughly until completely.

Combined.

Use immediately or store in an airtight container until ready to use.

Chipotle Chili Seasoning

Loria Flynn

1 Tbsp. chili powder
1 tsp. ground cumin
¼ tsp. cayenne pepper
½ tsp. chipotle pepper powder
¼ tsp. garlic powder
½ tsp. onion powder
½ tsp. black pepper

Ina sm. bowl add all spices. Mix thoroughly until completely combined.

Use immediately or store in an airtight container until ready to use.

Sweet and Spicy BBQ Sauce

Johnny Flynn

1 (15oz.) can tomato sauce.
1 (6oz.) can tomato paste.
¼ c. Worcestershire sauce
¼ c. apple cider vinegar
3 Tbsp. honey
3 cloves garlic, minced.
½ tsp. chipotle pepper powder
1 tsp. black pepper

Heat a lg. saucepan over med. Add all ingredients. Mix thoroughly until completely combined. Simmer 10 – 12 mins. Or until sauce is heated through. Use immediately or refrigerate in an airtight container up to 5 days.

Candied Apples

Loria Flynn

3 c. sugar
1 c. light corn syrup
1 ½tsp. red food coloring
12 popsicle sticks
12 med. apples
1 c. chopped nuts.

Combine sugar, syrup, water and food coloring in saucepan cook over med. heat until the mixture looks like wet cracks 8 to 10 mins. Turn heat to low. Stick a popsicle stick into each apple at the stem and dip each apple into the saucepan roll in the nuts, place om wax paper to cool and harden.

Garlic Butter

Loria Flynn

½ c. butter
½ to 1 garlic clove, minced.
1 tsp. parsley

In sm. bowl cream butter until very creamy blend in garlic and parsley.

Fresh Tarter Sauce

Loria Flynn

½ c. sour cream
½ c. mayo
1 tsp. lemon juice
2 Tbsp. onion finely chopped.
1 Tbsp. fresh parsley finely chopped.

Blend all ingredients thoroughly and place in a sm. bowl cover and put in refrigerator until cold.

BBQ Sauce

Loria Flynn

2 qt. katsup
¼ c. liquid smoke
¼ c. Worcestershire sauce
2 c. brown sugar
½ tsp. Tabasco sauce
1 sm. onion finely chopped.
2 cloves garlic, minced.

Mix and heat on low temp. for 20 to 0 mins. Onion finely chopped and garlic minced.

Chive butter

Loria Flynn

½ c. butter

3 Tbsp. chives chopped.

2 Tbsp. parsley chopped.

¼ tsp. salt

Dash cayenne pepper(if desired)

In sm. bowl cream butter very well, blind in remaining ingredients mix well.

Seasoned Butter

Loria Flynn

1 c. butter
3 Tbsp. mined parley
1 tsp. garlic powder
1 tsp. onion powder
½ tsp. pepper
2 Tbsp. lemon juice

In sm. bowl cream better well. Beat in remaining ingredients cover and refrigerate.

Butter syrup

Sarah Morrison

1c. evaporated milk
2 c. sugar
1 Tbsp. butter
1 tsp. vanilla

Combine milk, sugar, and butter.

In a sm. saucepan, bring to a boil add ½ tsp. vanilla stir. Serve warm.

Grace's pancake syrup

Grace Head

1 Tbsp. molasses
1 tsp. maple flavoring
½ tsp. butter flavoring
1 c. water
2 c. sugar

Bring 1 cup water to a boil add 2 cups sugar stir until dissolved add other 3 ingredients simmer to desired consistency. Serve warm.

Johnny's special marinade sauce
Johnny Flynn

1 c. 57 sauce

1 c. yellow mustard

⅓ c. tabasco sauce

1 c. A1 sauce

½ c. garlic powder

1c. Worcestershire sauce

¼ c. honey if desired

Mix all together and let set for 1 hr. mixing often to make sure it is all mixed. well together.

Johnny's Grilling Sauce

Johnny Flynn

1 c. 57 sauce
1 c. Yellow Mustard
⅓ c. tabasco sauce
1c. A1 sauce
½ c. garlic powder
1 c. Worcestershire sauce

Let set 1 hr. steering accusingly.

OTHER RECIPES

᭦᭦ FOOD QUANTITIES FOR 25, 50, AND 100 SERVINGS ᭦᭦

FOOD	25 Servings	50 Servings	100 Servings
Rolls	4 doz.	8 doz.	16 doz.
Bread	50 slices or 3 1-lb. loaves	100 slices or 6 1-lb. loaves	200 slices or 12 1-lb. loaves
Butter	½ lb.	¾ to 1 lb.	1½ lb.
Mayonnaise	1 c.	2 to 3 c.	4 to 6 c.
Mixed filling for sandwiches (meat, eggs, fish)	1½ qt.	2½ to 3 qt.	5 to 6 qt.
Mixed filling (sweet-fruit)	1 qt.	1¾ to 2 qt.	2 ½ to 4 qt.
Jams & preserves	1½ lb.	3 lb.	6 lb.
Crackers	1½ lb.	3 lb.	6 lb.
Cheese (2 oz. per serving)	3 lb.	6 lb.	12 lb.
Soup	1½ gal.	3 gal.	6 gal.
Salad dressings	1 pt.	2½ pt.	½ gal.

■ Meat, Poultry, or Fish

FOOD	25 Servings	50 Servings	100 Servings
Wieners (beef)	6½ lb.	13 lb.	25 lb.
Hamburger	9 lb.	18 lb.	35 lb.
Turkey or chicken	13 lb.	25 to 35 lb.	50 to 75 lb.
Fish, large whole (round)	13 lb.	25 lb.	50 lb.
Fish, fillets or steaks	7½ lb.	15 lb.	30 lb.

■ Salads, Casseroles, Vegetables

FOOD	25 Servings	50 Servings	100 Servings
Potato salad	4¼ qt.	2¼ gal.	4½ gal.
Scalloped potatoes	4½ qt. or 1 12x20" pan	8½ qt.	17 qt.
Mashed potatoes	9 lb.	18-20 lb.	25-35 lb.
Spaghetti	1¼ gal.	2½ gal.	5 gal.
Baked beans	¾ gal.	1¼ gal.	2½ gal.
Jello salad	¾ gal.	1¼ gal.	2½ gal.
Canned vegetables	1 #10 can	2½ #10 cans	4 #10 cans

■ Fresh Vegetables

FOOD	25 Servings	50 Servings	100 Servings
Lettuce (for salads)	4 heads	8 heads	15 heads
Carrots (3 oz. or ½ c.)	6¼ lb.	12½ lb.	25 lb.
Tomatoes	3-5 lb.	7-10 lb.	14-20 lb.

■ Desserts

FOOD	25 Servings	50 Servings	100 Servings
Watermelon	37½ lb.	75 lb.	150 lb.
Fruit cup (½ c. per serving)	3 qt.	6 qt.	12 qt.
Cake	1 10x12" sheet cake	1 12x20" sheet cake	2 12x20" sheet cakes
	1½ 10" layer cakes	3 10" layer cakes	6 10" layer cakes
Whipping cream	¾ pt.	1½ to 2 pt.	3 pt.

■ Ice Cream

FOOD	25 Servings	50 Servings	100 Servings
Brick	3¼ qt.	6½ qt.	12½ qt.
Bulk	2¼ qt.	4½ qt. or 1¼ gal.	9 qt. or 2½ gal.

■ Beverages

FOOD	25 Servings	50 Servings	100 Servings
Coffee	½ lb. and 1½ gal. water	1 lb. and 3 gal. water	2 lb. and 6 gal. water
Tea	1/12 lb. and 1½ gal. water	1/6 lb. and 3 gal. water	1/3 lb. and 6 gal. water
Lemonade	10 to 15 lemons, 1½ gal. water	20 to 30 lemons, 3 gal. water	40 to 60 lemons, 6 gal. water

⟿ EQUIVALENT CHART ⟾

3 tsp.	1 Tbsp.
2 Tbsp.	⅛ c.
4 Tbsp.	¼ c.
8 Tbsp.	½ c.
16 Tbsp.	1 c.
5 Tbsp. + 1 tsp.	⅓ c.
12 Tbsp.	¾ c.
4 oz.	½ c.
8 oz.	1 c.
16 oz.	1 lb.
1 oz.	2 Tbsp. fat or liquid
2 c.	1 pt.
2 pt.	1 qt.
1 qt.	4 c.
⅝ c.	½ c. + 2 Tbsp.
⅞ c.	¾ c. + 2 Tbsp.
1 jigger	1½ fl. oz. (3 Tbsp.)
8 to 10 egg whites	1 c.
12 to 14 egg yolks	1 c.
1 c. unwhipped cream	2 c. whipped
1 lb. shredded American cheese	4 c.

¼ lb. crumbled Bleu cheese	1 c.
1 lemon	3 Tbsp. juice
1 orange	⅓ c. juice
1 lb. unshelled walnuts	1½ to 1¾ c. shelled
2 c. fat	1 lb.
1 lb. butter	2 c. or 4 sticks
2 c. granulated sugar	1 lb.
3½-4 c. unsifted powdered sugar	1 lb.
2¼ c. packed brown sugar	1 lb.
4 c. sifted flour	1 lb.
4½ c. cake flour	1 lb.
3½ c. unsifted whole wheat flour	1 lb.
4 oz. (1 to 1¼ c.) uncooked macaroni	2¼ c. cooked
7 oz. spaghetti	4 c. cooked
4 oz. (1½ to 2 c.) uncooked noodles	2 c. cooked
28 saltine crackers	1 c. crumbs
4 slices bread	1 c. crumbs
14 square graham crackers	1 c. crumbs
22 vanilla wafers	1 c. crumbs

⟿ SUBSTITUTIONS FOR A MISSING INGREDIENT ⟾

1 square **chocolate** (1 ounce) = 3 or 4 tablespoons cocoa plus ½ tablespoon fat
1 tablespoon **cornstarch** (for thickening) = 2 tablespoons flour
1 cup sifted **all-purpose flour** = 1 cup plus 2 tablespoons sifted cake flour
1 cup sifted **cake flour** = 1 cup minus 2 tablespoons sifted all-purpose flour
1 teaspoon **baking powder** = ¼ teaspoon baking soda plus ½ teaspoon cream of tartar
1 cup **sour milk** = 1 cup sweet milk into which 1 tablespoon vinegar or lemon juice has been stirred
1 cup **sweet milk** = 1 cup sour milk or buttermilk plus ½ teaspoon baking soda
¾ cup **cracker crumbs** = 1 cup bread crumbs
1 cup **cream, sour, heavy** = ⅓ cup butter and ⅔ cup milk in any sour milk recipe
1 teaspoon **dried herbs** = 1 tablespoon fresh herbs
1 cup **whole milk** = ½ cup evaporated milk and ½ cup water or 1 cup reconstituted nonfat dry milk and 1 tablespoon butter
2 ounces **compressed yeast** = 3 (¼ ounce) packets of dry yeast
1 tablespoon **instant minced onion, rehydrated** = 1 small fresh onion
1 tablespoon **prepared mustard** = 1 teaspoon dry mustard
⅛ teaspoon **garlic powder** = 1 small pressed clove of garlic
1 lb. **whole dates** = 1½ cups, pitted and cut
3 medium **bananas** = 1 cup mashed
3 cups **dry corn flakes** = 1 cup crushed
10 **miniature marshmallows** = 1 large marshmallow

⟿ OVEN CHART ⟾

Very slow oven	250° to 300°F.
Slow oven	300° to 325°F.
Moderate oven	325° to 375°F.
Medium hot oven	375° to 400°F.
Hot oven	400° to 450°F.
Very hot oven	450° to 500°F.

⟿ CONTENT OF CANS ⟾

Of the different sizes of cans used by commercial canners, the most common are:

Size:	Average Contents
8 oz.	1 cup
Picnic	1¼ cups
No. 300	1¾ cups
No. 1 tall	2 cups
No. 303	2 cups
No. 2	2½ cups
No. 2½	3½ cups
No. 3	4 cups
No. 10	12 to 13 cups

382

ᗥ A HANDY SPICE AND HERB GUIDE ᗧ

- **ALLSPICE** – a pea-sized fruit that grows in Mexico, Jamaica, Central and South America. Its delicate flavor resembles a blend of cloves, cinnamon, and nutmeg. USES: (Whole) Pickles, meats, boiled fish, gravies; (Ground) Puddings, relishes, fruit preserves, baking.
- **BASIL** – the dried leaves and stems of an herb grown in the United States and North Mediterranean area. Has an aromatic, leafy flavor. USES: For flavoring tomato dishes and tomato paste; also use in cooked peas, squash, snap beans; sprinkle chopped over lamb chops and poultry.
- **BAY LEAVES** – the dried leaves of an evergreen grown in the eastern Mediterranean countries. Has a sweet, herbaceous floral spice note. USES: For pickling, stews, for spicing sauces and soup. Also use with a variety of meats and fish.
- **CARAWAY** – the seed of a plant grown in the Netherlands. Flavor that combines the tastes of anise and dill. USES: For the cordial Kummel, baking breads; often added to sauerkraut, noodles, cheese spreads. Also adds zest to French fried potatoes, and canned asparagus.
- **CINNAMON** – Obtained from the inner bark of several tree species; native to India, Sri Lanka, and Bangladesh. USES: Carrots, squash, sweet potatoes, lamb, stir fries; beverages; pickling, known for its flavoring role in breads, fruit and a variety of desserts.
- **CURRY POWDER** – a ground blend of ginger, turmeric, fenugreek seed, as many as 16 to 20 spices. USES: For all Indian curry recipes such as lamb, chicken, and rice, eggs, vegetables, and curry puffs.
- **DILL** – the small, dark seed of the dill plant grown in India, having a clean, aromatic taste. USES: Dill is a predominant seasoning in pickling recipes; also adds pleasing flavor to sauerkraut, potato salad, cooked macaroni, and green apple pie.
- **MACE** – the dried covering around the nutmeg seed. Its flavor is similar to nutmeg, but with a fragrant, delicate difference. USES: (Whole) For pickling, fish, fish sauce, stewed fruit.(Ground) Delicious in baked goods, pastries, and doughnuts, adds unusual flavor to chocolate desserts.
- **MARJORAM** – an herb of the mint family, grown in France and Chile. Has a minty-sweet flavor. USES: In beverages, jellies, and to flavor soups, stews, fish, sauces. Also excellent to sprinkle on lamb while roasting.
- **OREGANO** – a plant of the mint family and a species of marjoram of which the dried leaves are used to make an herb seasoning. USES: An excellent flavoring for any tomato dish, especially pizza, chili con carne, and Italian specialties.
- **PAPRIKA** – a mild, sweet red pepper growing in Spain, Central Europe, and the United States. Slightly aromatic and prized for brilliant red color. USES: A colorful garnish for pale foods, and for seasoning Chicken Paprika, Hungarian Goulash, salad dressings.
- **POPPY** – the seed of a flower grown in Holland. Has a rich fragrance and crunchy, nut-like flavor. USES: Excellent as a topping for breads, rolls, and cookies. Also delicious in buttered noodles.
- **ROSEMARY** – an herb (like a curved pine needle) grown in France, Spain, and Portugal, and having a sweet fresh taste. USES: In lamb dishes, in soups, stews, and to sprinkle on beef before roasting.
- **SAGE** – the leaf of a shrub grown in Greece, Yugoslavia, and Albania. Flavor is camphoraceous and minty. USES: For meat and poultry stuffing, sausages, meat loaf, hamburgers, stews, and salads.
- **THYME** – the leaves and stems of a shrub grown in France and Spain. Has a strong, distinctive flavor. USES: For poultry seasoning, croquettes, fricassees, and fish dishes. Also tasty on fresh sliced tomatoes.
- **TURMERIC** – a root of the ginger family, grown in India, Haiti, Jamaica, and Peru, having a mild, ginger-pepper flavor. USES: As a flavoring and coloring in prepared mustard and in combination with mustard as a flavoring for meats, dressings, salads.

✌ TEMPERATURE TESTS FOR CANDY MAKING ☜

There are two different methods of determining when candy has been cooked to the proper consistency. One is by using a candy thermometer in order to record degrees, the other is by using the cold water test. The chart below will prove useful in helping to follow candy recipes:

TYPE OF CANDY	DEGREES	COLD WATER
Fondant, Fudge	234 - 238°	Soft Ball
Divinity, Caramels	245 - 248°	Firm Ball
Taffy	265 - 270°	Hard Ball
Butterscotch	275 - 280°	Light Crack
Peanut Brittle	285 - 290°	Hard Crack
Caramelized Sugar	310 - 321°	Caramelized

In using the cold water test, use a fresh cupful of cold water for each test. When testing, remove the candy from the fire and pour about ½ teaspoon of candy into the cold water. Pick the candy up in the fingers and roll into a ball if possible.

In the SOFT BALL TEST the candy will roll into a soft ball which quickly loses its shape when removed from the water.

In the FIRM BALL TEST the candy will roll into a firm, but not hard ball. It will flatten out a few minutes after being removed from the water.

In the HARD BALL TEST the candy will roll into a hard ball which has lost almost all plasticity and will roll around on a plate on removal from the water.

In the LIGHT CRACK TEST the candy will form brittle threads which will soften on removal from the water.

In the HARD CRACK TEST the candy will form brittle threads in the water which will remain brittle after being removed from the water.

In CARAMELIZING the sugar first melts then becomes a golden brown. It will form a hard brittle ball in cold water.

❦ APPLE VARIETIES ❧

NAME	SEASON	COLOR	FLAVOR/ TEXTURE	EATING	PIE
Astrachan	July-Aug	Yellow/ Greenish Red	Sweet	Good	Good
Baldwin	Oct-Jan	Red/ Yellowish	Mellow	Fair	Fair
Cortland	Oct-Jan	Green/Purple	Mild, tender	Excel.	Excel.
Delicious, Red	Sept-June	Scarlet	Sweet, crunchy	Excel.	Good
Delicious, Golden	Sept-May	Yellow	Sweet, semifirm	Excel.	Excel.
Empire	Sept-Nov	Red	Sweet, crisp	Excel.	Good
Fameuse	Sept-Nov	Red	Mild, crisp	Excel.	Fair
Granny Smith	Apr-July	Green	Tart, crisp	V. Good	V. Good
Gravenstein	July-Sept	Green w/red stripes	Tart, crisp	Good	Good
Ida Red	Oct	Red	Rich	Good	Good
Jonathan	Sept-Jan	Brilliant red Tart,	tender, crisp	V. Good	V. Good
Macoun	Oct-Nov	Dark red	Tart, juicy, crisp	Excel.	Good
McIntosh	Sept-June	Green to red	Slightly tart, tender, juicy	Excel.	Excel.
Newtown Pippin	Sept-June	Green to red	Slightly tart, firm	V. Good	Excel.
Northern Spy	Oct	Red	Crisp, tart	V. Good	V. Good
Rhode Island Greening	Sept-Nov	Green	Very tart, firm	Poor	Excel.
Rome Beauty	Oct-June	Red	Tart, firm, slightly dry	Good	V. Good
Stayman-Winesap	Oct-Mar	Red	Semifirm, sweet, spicy	V. Good	Good
Winesap	Oct-June	Red	Slightly tart, firm, spicy	Excel.	Good
Yellow Transparent	July-Aug	Yellow	Tart, soft	Poor	Excel.

❧ TIPS FOR THE PERFECT BREAD ☙

For the best bread, always use fresh ingredients at room temperature.

Use a dry measuring cup to measure dry ingredients and a glass or plastic liquid measuring cup to measure liquids.

Do not scoop flour with a measuring cup or too much flour will be used making the loaf heavy. Instead, use a spoon to lift the flour out of the container and into the measuring cup, then level the top with a flat edge.

Bread gets its lightness from yeast (or soda in quick non-yeast breads) so sifting of the dry ingredients is not necessary when making bread.

Be precise in following the recipe's directions for preheating and baking.

Oven temperatures may vary so use an oven thermometer for accuracy. Check loaves about 10 minutes before the recipe says they should be done.

Cool bread on a wire rack to prevent it from getting soggy from steam accumulating on the bottom of the pan. Wait at least 15 minutes after removing yeast bread from the oven before cutting so that the crust doesn't tear. Quick breads cut better the next day.

❧ Yeast Breads ☙

Kneading – Place dough in a ball on a floured surface and, with floured hands, flatten dough and fold towards you. With the heel of hands, push the dough away with a rolling motion. Rotate dough a quarter turn and repeat the "fold, push, and turn" steps until the dough is smooth and elastic, about 4 to 10 minutes.

Resting/Rising – Place kneaded dough in a greased bowl and cover the top loosely with a damp, clean cloth or plastic wrap sprayed with nonstick cooking spray. Set in a warm, draft-free place until the dough is doubled in bulk, or until the tips of two fingers lightly and quickly pressed ½ inch into the dough leave an impression.

Place baking pans several inches apart on the center oven rack. Remove baked bread from pans immediately after baking. Tap the bottom or side of the loaf and, if it sounds hollow, the bread is done.

❧ Quick Breads ☙

Mix dry ingredients in a large bowl and wet ingredients in a medium bowl. Add wet ingredients to dry and stir only until combined. Mixture should be lumpy. Overmixing causes peaks and tunnels in the loaves and tough texture.

If shortening is used, cut into dry ingredients with a pastry blender or two knives in scissor fashion.

For small muffins, fill cups $^2/_3$ full; medium muffins, fill cups almost to the top; huge muffins, fill cups completely full and grease top of pan. Fill any empty muffin cups halfway with water.

Check quick breads 10 to 15 minutes before baking time is up. Cover with foil if top is browning too much. Test for doneness with a toothpick.

❧ Whole Grains and Non-Wheat Flours ☙

Whole-grain breads do not rise as high as breads made with all-white flour. Store whole-grain flours, wheat germ, bran, nuts, and seeds in the refrigerator or freezer. Pine nuts, hazelnuts, and almonds will be more flavorful when lightly toasted before adding to the dough.

Wheat germ increases the nutritional value but inhibits the gluten action so do not use more than 2 tablespoons for every 2 cups of flour. Use old-fashioned rolled oats, not "quick oats" in bread recipes.

Whole grain flour may be substituted one-to-one without making other changes in muffins, scones, and quick breads. For yeast breads that need to rise, substitute whole wheat flour for half of the all-purpose flour without making any other changes. For 100% whole wheat flour, add an extra 2 teaspoons liquid per cup of whole wheat flour, and let the dough rest 25 minutes before kneading.

COMMON BAKING DISHES AND PANS

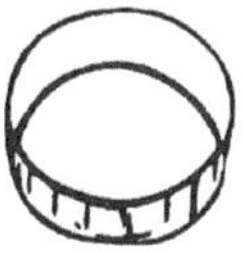

Spring Form Pan

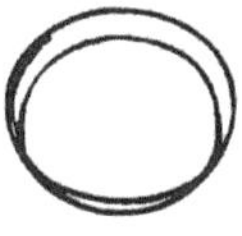

Layer Cake or Pie Pan

Ring Mold

Baking or Square Pan

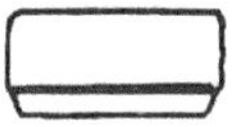

Loaf Pan

Brioche Pan

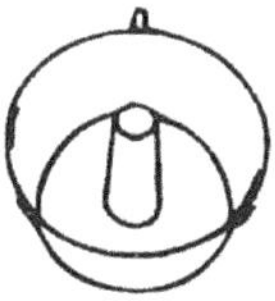

Angel Cake Pan

Bundt Tube

Equivalent Dishes

4-CUP BAKING DISH
= 9" pie plate
= 8" x 1¼" layer cake pan
= 7⅜" x 3⅝" x 2¼" loaf pan

6-CUP BAKING DISH
= 8" or 9" x 1½" layer cake pan
= 10" pie pan
= 8½" x 3⅝" x 2⅝" loaf pan

8-CUP BAKING DISH
= 8" x 8" x 2" square pan
= 11" x 7" x 1½" baking pan
= 9" x 5" x 3" loaf pan

10-CUP BAKING DISH
= 9" x 9" x 2" square pan
= 11¾" x 7½" x 1¾" baking pan
= 15" x 10" x 1" flat jelly roll pan

12-CUP BAKING DISH OR MORE
= 13½" x 8½" x 2" glass baking dish
= 13" x 9" x 2" metal baking pan
= 14" x 10½" x 2½" roasting pan

Total Volume of Pans

TUBE PANS
7½" x 3" Bundt tube	6 cups
9" x 3½" fancy or Bundt tube	9 cups
9" x 3½" angel cake pan	12 cups
10" x 3¾" Bundt tube	12 cups
9" x 3½" fancy tube mold	12 cups
10" x 4" fancy tube mold	16 cups
10" x 4" angel cake pan	18 cups

SPRING FORM PANS
8" x 3" pan	12 cups
9" x 3" pan	16 cups

RING MOLDS
8½" x 2¼" mold	4½ cups
9¼" x 2¾" mold	8 cups

BRIOCHE PAN
9½" x 3¼" pan	8 cups

✌️ COOKING SUGGESTIONS ☙

To toast coconut for cakes, put in pie pan and place in moderate oven. Stir often from edges, to brown evenly.

Flour should be sifted once before measuring. Fill the cup without packing.

Do not grease the sides of cake pans, grease only the bottom. When beating egg whites do not tap beater on bowl of egg whites. The jarring of beater will cause the whites to lose a great deal of their fluffiness. The beater should be tapped on the hand to clear off the whites.

Rub the bottom of the soup cup with a sliced whole garlic to accent the flavor of Navy Bean Soup.

Eggs should be at least three days old before using in cakes.

SLOW OVEN. . . . . 300 to 325 degrees
MODERATE OVEN . . . . 325 to 375 degrees
HOT OVEN . . . . 400 to 450 degrees
VERY HOT OVEN . . . . 450 to 500 degrees

When making cake icing or candy consisting of milk or cream and sugar, add one teaspoon of ordinary table syrup for each cup of sugar used. Boil in the usual way. Your finished product will be much smoother and not so apt to become sugary.

FAMILY PICTURES

Lightning Source UK Ltd.
Milton Keynes UK
UKHW011843200123
415716UK00013B/168/J